The Unofficial Guidebook To

Surviving Life With Teenagers

Edited by
Tiffany O'Connor & Lyndee Brown

Copyright © 2019 HCCR Books
All rights reserved.

No Part of this book may be used, reproduced, or transmitted in any matter whatsoever, including but not limited to electronic or mechanical means, photocopying, recording, or by any information storage and retrieval system without written permission in writing from the author, except in the case of brief quotations embodied in critical articles and reviews.

ISBN: 0960091319
ISBN-13: 978-0960091317 (HCCR Books)

This book is dedicated to the children of each and every writer who contributed a story in this book. Without all of you this book would not have been possible.

YOUR PARENTS LOVE YOU VERY MUCH!

Contents

Foreword	
Dear Teenage Daughter, When I Let You Fall	2
Honesty is the Best Policy	6
The Day My Son Ran Away	13
Lessons from My Tween Son	17
My Battle Call	20
A Miracle at the County Fair	25
This Is What Life with a Teenage Daughter Is Sometimes Like	30
My Best Parenting Advice: Buy Post-it Notes	33
Baby, You Can Drive My Car	36
The Teen Years – Does All This Sitting Make My Butt Look Big?	42
Building Trust with No Consequence Conversations	46
From Eye Rolls to Sleepovers, We're in this Together	51
The Glorious Thing That Happens to Every Teen Mom	55
Enough	58
Hey, Fifteen	61
Parenting While Chronically Ill: Maybe You Did Enough	65
Goody-Two-Shoes Barbie	69
I'm His Mom and Not His Sister	74

I Forgot To Raise Him to Be a Man	79
His First Middle School Dance	83
Moving Toward Adulthood	87
The Basic Dad	91
I'm Ready When You Are	96
Parenting a Struggling Teen	101
The Miracle of the Age Gap	105
The Teenage Years Are Tough	110
About the Authors	114
Letter from the Editors	121

FOREWORD

Melissa Fenton

*"Internet Searches Moms of Teens Do:
Car insurance discounts.
How to argue with crazy people.
Early college enrollment.
Laundry odor remover.
When do teens become rational?
Anger management skills before you stab someone. Conversation starters for people who don't want to talk.
Reducing your grocery bill.
Finding joy in chaotic times.
Retiring in Tahiti" ~ 4BoysMother*

While in the throes of mothering through terrible, toddler tantrums and endless potty training accidents, I recall thinking to myself, "I can't wait until they are teenagers and totally self-sufficient!"

And then while in the throes of mothering through the terrible teen years and endless eye-rolling, in the ultimate twist of irony, I recall thinking to myself, "I'd give anything right now for my biggest problem to be a missed nap and poopy pants."

(And then right after that thought, I called my mother and apologized for my teen years.)

Nobody prepared me for the mentally exhausting toll parenting teenagers would burden me with, nor did I think the struggles

Tiffany O'Connor

I found myself having would be something I wouldn't feel comfortable sharing with other mothers. For some reason, when we parent difficult toddlers, we talk about it endlessly with friends and without shame. The same does not happen when we parent teenagers, and it makes many moms think they're doing it wrong, and only their teens are hard.

But the truth is, we're all being sucker-punched daily by these new hormonal (and very different) people we wake up one day and find ourselves living with, and it is only by sharing our struggles with other moms in the same situation that we (and the teens!) are able to survive. And by sharing our struggles, I mean laughing about it. Because if we didn't laugh? Well, I'm certain none of us would make it to high school graduation!

Dear Teenage Daughter, When I Let You Fall

Whitney Fleming

"If you are having a good morning with your teen, do not— I repeat DO NOT—walk into their room, check their grades, or look in the sink after they leave. You just enjoy that feeling as long as you can." ~Playdates on Fridays

Dear Daughter,

I've spent a great deal of your life lifting you up. It started innocently enough. I held your hands high when you were learning to walk on unsteady feet. I hoisted you up to my hip when the ducks got to close to our picnic table at the zoo, and you could no longer control your fear. I've walked behind you, helping to pick up your toys and clothes and school work.

As you grew older, I continued to hold you up. I took your lunch to school a few times and helped too much on projects when you complained you were stumped. I picked up your room because I thought you were busy and let you quit a team because of the behavior of others. I bought you a new soccer ball when you lost your other one right before practice, fearing you may get in trouble with the coach.

I've always lifted you up, smoothing your path as you made your way in this world, mitigating the pain you might experience. I wanted to help you succeed, help you to be your best.

But now, we've hit the teenage years, and life is barreling at us.

You are faced with difficult choices every day, and my fears magnified. You desperately seek independence while I struggle to keep some control.

And I worry.

Will you learn the skills you need to succeed in this world?

Will you live life to your potential or merely get through a day?

Will you have the resilience to get back up if life knocks you down?

Recently, I watched as you walked out the door to school, forgetting an important project on the kitchen counter. I knew you might get a failing grade, I knew the teacher might deem you irresponsible, reflecting poorly on me. And although every fiber of my being wanted to protect you from pain, from embarrassment, from any negative impact on your future, I did not bring it to you. I know you must learn to be more responsible, must learn how to deal with these situations yourself.

So, I let you fall.

I put my arm tightly around you when you came home from school on a rainy Friday, upset about a disagreement with your friends. I cringed when I heard the words that were said; I flinched at the anger portrayed by all involved. I listened and nodded and wiped away the tears. My instinct was to call up your friends or their parents, to explain the misunderstanding that was so clear in my eyes. My anxiety soared at the fear of your social distress. But your relationships are your own, and it's not my job to make the hurt go away.

So, I hugged you, then let you fall.

When I knew you wanted to try out for a play that I didn't think you had a chance to make, I longed to shield you from the inevitable pain, to steer you down a different path that was more likely to yield success. Instead, I drove you to the auditions each day and took you out for ice cream to celebrate trying a new thing. I didn't take away that experience or the disappointment that came with it.

As hard as it was, I let you fall.

Trust me, dear daughter, these decisions are not easy for me. I don't always feel confident about when to step in and when to let an event unfold. It is a scary thing not to know how you will handle a situation; it is difficult when I am sure you will feel pain. I know you don't understand my motives, why sometimes I hold you up, and sometimes I let you fall. I know you want to blame me or your teachers or your friends for your problems.
But I need you to know, dear daughter, that sometimes love and support means letting you fail. The consequences you experience are a gift, an opportunity to learn from your mistakes. You will never be prepared to face the world if I'm always lifting you up, you will never improve if you don't make mistakes. But letting you fall doesn't mean I'm abandoning you.

I will always encourage you with uplifting words, so you know your value and self-worth.

I will build up your self-esteem by focusing on your strengths.

And when life gets tough—which it will—I will ALWAYS be there to listen and guide you on your way.

We are all human, sweet girl, so we all make mistakes and stumble and fall from time to time. So, my dear daughter, I want you to feel the pain and the struggle of falling so you believe you can cope, so you can have the ability to navigate this world, so you know you can get back up on your own.

Tiffany O'Connor

I sighed as I walked into the kitchen this morning to get another cup of coffee and saw your gym uniform sitting in a plastic bag next to your science textbook. I looked at the clock to see if there was time to get it to you before classes started, knowing how hard you've worked to be more responsible this year. Just then, you burst through the door, grabbed your things on the counter, planted a kiss on my cheek and bolted.

I smiled as I looked out the window as your slight figure raced down the sidewalk and leaped up the steps of the yellow school bus.

Watching you fall, sweet girl is so very hard. But getting to see you get back up and soar…well, that's a thing of beauty.

Honesty is the Best Policy
Tiffany O'Connor

"I texted my teenage son multiple times today and was getting really annoyed that he wasn't answering...and then I remembered that I grounded him from his phone a few days ago and it was sitting on my dresser all day." ~#Lifewithboys

My fifteen-year-old son called me the other day while I was at a writing conference to talk to me about some personal things that were going on in his life and to ask me for advice. I'm always amazed when he does stuff like that at how open and honest he is. I am not stupid enough to think that he tells his dad and me everything, but I think we know about 80% of what is going on in his life. He has shown time and time again that we can trust him to come to us and tell us about things when the load is too heavy for him to bear alone or he doesn't know the best decision...especially the really important stuff

I am not one of those super cool moms that kids want to hang out with (I'm more of a blast Taylor Swift in the car while singing off-key and doing lame dance moves kind of mom.) I am definitely not the world's best mom either (the Mom of the Year voting committee permanently removed my name from the running the year my oldest drove his gas-powered scooter into his elementary school, and the principal had to hire a hazmat team to remove the carpet...ok actually it was probably removed the second day of his life when I dropped him off the couch on to his head.)

So why does my teenager call me up to tell me things?

Tiffany O'Connor

I believe that the reason he talks to me is because my husband and I have developed a policy where we are completely transparent, open, and honest with him about our lives. Over the past few years, my husband and I have told our teenage son almost everything about our past. We have told him what we regretted, what we didn't regret, and the times our decisions good or bad changed the course of our lives or the lives of the people around us in unforeseen ways.

It was extremely difficult the first few times I had to tell my baby boy about mistakes that I made or things that I did in the past that I wasn't proud of. However, as we started having hard conversations with him, I realized that he was actually listening to us and engaging in those conversations. It is one thing to have your parent say, "Don't do drugs because they are bad for you" and it is another to have your parent say, "These are the experiences that I had with drugs, why I did them, exactly what it was like, what I regret, what your family history is with drugs and the honest reasons why I really want you to stay away from them."

Obviously, you can't expect your child to completely listen to you or to learn from your mistakes, but you can give them enough information that if they even listened to half of what you told them they could make educated decisions knowing and understanding most of the possible risks and consequences that they might face.

My original fear was that I would lose his respect or love if I told him everything about me. I thought about *The Wizard of Oz* and how when Dorothy removed the curtain and discovered that the Great and Powerful Oz was a fraud and nothing more than a sideshow magician, she was angry and disappointed with him. It is one thing to know that you are not on the short list for Mom of the Year because your toddler once drank lighter fluid while you were not paying attention and poison control had to instruct you to keep him away from open flames, and it is another thing to actually tell that to the same toddler who somehow survived to become a teenager.

However, then I realized that if you are not honest with your kids, then you are allowing them to believe a false narrative…one where you could never understand what they are going through.

Sometimes being honest with your teenager is hard. Sometimes they will throw your past in your face because teenagers can be moody, selfish brats…but most of the time it makes them see you as a human who is flawed and will understand them instead of a perfect parent they don't want to disappoint. My son has the freedom to ask us for our opinions and be open and honest with us because he knows we have been there and won't judge him. He knows that he can trust us. He knows that we will always be proud of him even if we don't like the decisions that he makes and that we will always love him unconditionally no matter what.

I couldn't be open and honest with my parents as a teenager because I didn't trust them, I believed that they would judge me, and I didn't think that they loved me unconditionally.

In high school, I was the perfect teenager on paper; Honors Student, Captain of the Varsity Cheerleading team, Sports Editor of the Yearbook, President of the Student Council, Co-Captain of the Girls Varsity Swim team, Captain of The Girls Varsity Track team, and I was our local cities Lifeguard of the Year. In my free time, I planned regional galas for Make-a-Wish, volunteered at a Children's hospital, tutored underclassmen, and spent my evenings reading classic novels and watching *Star Trek* reruns.

Despite all of that, I never felt good enough. I never felt like my parents were proud of me.

Excellence in school was just expected of me. My mother would use the term "scholastically intelligent" to explain away my good grades and high standardized test scores. I can't tell you how many times I sat at dinner and listened to her tell someone that I was "scholastically intelligent, but that I didn't have any common sense." I felt like she believed that school was just easy for me, and the fact that I lacked real-life skills was a better barometer of how little I would contribute to society in the future.

My athletic attributes were also worthless when it came to impressing my parents. Unlike academics, it was obvious that I was not a natural when it came to athletics. The joke in my family was that I did swimming and track because I couldn't do any 'REAL SPORTS'…you know sports that involved a ball and actually mattered. When I told my mother that I was going to try out for cheerleading, she warned me that I probably wouldn't make the team. I was uncoordinated, clumsy, and dowdy. When I did make the team, she commented that it was most likely because all of the really talented girls were on the dance squad like my older sister.

I remember standing in the mirror the first time that I tried on my uniform…looking at my 5ft 7in 137lb body and pinching what little fat I could between my fingers and wishing that I could cut it off. I spent most of my early teen years covering my body up in baggy boyfriend jeans and oversized t-shirts because I felt fat and was constantly teased by my family for my 'bubble butt' and my chest that was so flat that 'I made the wall jealous.'

For the majority of my youth, I believed that my parents were perfect and that I would never live up to their high expectations. I had grown up hearing the stories about how my mom was a gorgeous, popular perfect student in high school who selflessly gave up her chance to do things like cheerleading to take care of my grandmother who had cancer and her younger brothers.

My father was a hardworking kid who was well-liked by everyone and had almost become famous because of his musical talents before he joined the military and proudly served in Vietnam. They met, had the perfect love story, and got married. He worked his way up the corporate ladder without a college degree and worked a second job as a karaoke DJ at night so that he would have the money to make sure that all of his kids could afford to attain one.

They were good Catholics, who were very against drugs, underage drinking, premarital sex, and swearing. They were strict about curfews, extremely judgmental towards people they deemed themselves better than, and didn't hide their disapproval when their children did something they disliked. Our family motto was, "No lying, cheating, stealing, or hurting your brothers and sisters." I truly believed that my parents NEVER did any of those things.

When we became teenagers, my sister avoided their negative comments and judgments by lying to them and then doing whatever she wanted. She would tell my parents that we were going to the zoo and then I would spend the next three hours reading a book on the couch at her boyfriend's house while she hung out with him in his bedroom. My parents would go to the bar at night for my dad's second job, and my sister would drink and have boys over and then she would blame one of my younger siblings when something was found broken or missing. Sometimes she got caught…but most of the time she got away with it. I quickly learned that if I couldn't be perfect that faking perfection was the next best thing.

I stopped telling my parents about anything bad in my life.

I didn't tell them when I got bullied by a group of girls that I thought were my friends.

I didn't tell them when a close friend committed suicide and I believed that I was to blame.

I didn't tell them when I had a crush on a boy that was unrequited and I cried myself to sleep for a month.

I didn't tell them when I made a mistake like when I got a parking ticket, bounced a check, or stained my favorite shirt… instead, I would try to fix these things by myself to avoid their disappointment usually making the problem worse in the process.

I rarely went to parties, but if I did I would lie to them about where I was going… I knew that I wasn't going to drink or do drugs but I lied to them anyway because I figured that they would think I was bad for even wanting to go. There were even times when I put myself in bad positions and did things like sleep in my car when the friend whose house I was supposed to stay at ditched me to avoid going home and telling my parents what happened.

I would hide in my room for hours to avoid talking to them and when I did have to talk to them I would tell them half-truths or make up some ridiculous story to get them to leave me alone or let me do what I wanted to like I had seen my sister do.

It wasn't just the bad stuff…I also stopped telling them about a lot of the good things in my life too. Things like when I fell in love for the first time, what colleges I got accepted to, and the fact that all of my teachers kept telling me I needed to pursue writing and that I secretly dreamed of becoming an author.

I was a virtual stranger living in their home. They thought they knew me…but they didn't.

Honestly, they still don't really know me. My unhealthy pattern of being unable to honestly communicate with them continued into adulthood until our relationship was so toxic and messed up that it was healthier for me not to talk to them at all.

The sad thing is that all of this was avoidable. As an adult, I learned that none of the things I believed about my parents when I was a teenager were true. The truth was that they had a lot of secrets, had made a lot of mistakes, and had learned a lot of life lessons the hard way and if they had shared this with me when I was a teenager maybe things would have been different.

Maybe I would have felt comfortable enough to talk to them.

Maybe I never would have started to lie to them as a defense mechanism.

Maybe I wouldn't have felt so inadequate and unworthy.

Maybe I would have believed that they could love me unconditionally.

Maybe we would still have a relationship.

These maybes are why I am open and honest with my son. I don't want history to repeat itself.

If you are not honest with your teenager, they probably won't be honest with you.

If you don't let your teenagers know who you really are, you can't expect them to show you who they really are.

I don't want my son to think I am perfect…I want him to know without a shadow of a doubt that I will love every imperfect part of him perfectly.

The Day My Son Ran Away
Marcia Kester Doyle

"If you can survive raising teenagers, you can survive anything." ~Menopausal Mother

I thought I had the whole raising-responsible-teens thing down after surviving the ordeal with three of my four children. I was right there beside them in the trenches as they battled the Seven Dwarves of "Teenage-Dom": Moody, Impulsive, Dramatic, Insecure, Sensitive, Belligerent, and Indifferent. A healthy amount of love and parental guidance helped me survive the battle unscathed, and I took pride in sending each one off to college without an arrest record or a shotgun wedding.

Just when I thought it was safe to give myself a pat on the back, my youngest son proved that God has a sense of humor....and that the joke was on me.

Even as a toddler, there wasn't a baby gate, child proof lock or electric outlet that my boy couldn't break into. This was just a preview of what was to come in his teen years. My youngest son Jack is the reason behind the industrial-size bucket of "Grey-Be-Gone" hair dye that I used every three weeks, and the cause of daily nail-biting that left my hands looking like small rodents had been gnawing on my cuticles. I'm not exaggerating when I say that a typical morning with Jack usually involved matches, an aerosol can of hairspray and a plastic milk jug. He was a born daredevil who thought nothing of throwing potato bombs at our backyard fence or attaching a rolling office chair to the fender of his best friend's bike to be pushed down the highway.

As with any teen, boundaries needed to be set early on, but I also wanted to give Jack space during his formative years so that he could establish a sense of identity and independence. It wasn't long though before I discovered he was a magnet for trouble---something I didn't understand since my other teens were careful to avoid anything that involved school detentions, broken curfews, or (God forbid) handcuffs.

There were not enough parenting manuals in the world to teach me how to handle a thirteen-year-old boy who risked his health on a daily basis. During the God-awful middle school years, he insisted on wearing low slung jeans with the torn hems dragging on the ground in an attempt to fit in with the cool "gangsta" kids. I warned him that it wasn't a good idea, and sure enough, when he was late to class one morning, he ran to beat the bell and tripped over those pants. Off we went to the hospital to have a metal screw put into his fractured hip bone.

We bought him a bike in the hopes that it would keep his afternoons occupied and trouble-free, but within a year, he was accidentally struck twice by motorists. Like a cat with nine lives, he walked away both times with only bumps and bruises, and I was incredibly grateful that it hadn't been worse.

Shortly after he turned fourteen, and without any warning sign, Jack decided to run away from home rather than face the consequences of a poor report card. When he didn't return from school that afternoon, the world stopped on its axis. I was trapped inside every parent's worst nightmare; my child had disappeared without a trace. I didn't know if he had simply gone to a friend's house without telling me (something he'd never done before), if he'd run away voluntarily, or if he'd been abducted, which was a terrifying thought.

The police were called and immediately swarmed our street and the surrounding neighborhoods in search of my son. It was both horrifying and surreal to hear a helicopter circling above our home and see uniformed men with drug-sniffing dogs on our property. At one point, there were thirty people in my house, including the mayor, a county commissioner, and the school principal. As grateful as I was for all the love and support from the community, I just wanted my son to come home.

After spending several torturous hours pacing, crying, and begging God to bring my boy back safely, the police found him on a Greyhound Bus two hours from home, headed for Orlando. My immediate relief at hearing that he was safe quickly turned to anger over the anguish he'd put us through.

Once he was brought home, I decided to save my commentary until I knew his jumbled brain was ready to hear what I had to say. I simply hugged him and asked him to sleep on the couch nearby so that I could keep an eye on him. I tossed and turned that night, second guessing every decision I'd ever made as a parent. It dawned on me that even though I'd employed the same style of parenting on Jack that I had with my three older children, he required a completely different approach, and somehow I'd overlooked his needs.

Since that terrible day, my husband and I made major changes in our son's life by going with him to weekly therapy sessions and transferring him to a smaller school to alleviate the bullying he'd endured at his previous school. Prior to his running away, I had no idea that he was failing his classes or being teased by the other kids because he'd hid it so well. I'd missed all the signs, believing that his moodiness and belligerence were nothing more than typical teenage angst. But it went much deeper than that, and as a parent, I regretted that I'd been blind to his sensitivity and his inability to handle the stress at school.

In a way, I had to get reacquainted with Jack all over again, but the difference this time was that I did more listening and less talking when I was with him. A mutual respect grew between us, creating the strong bond that had been missing from our relationship before his troubles came to light.

Of course, there were still days when my boy challenged me and made me wish that I could either lobotomize him or trade him in for a house-trained Labrador, but I realized that this was a normal, knee-jerk reaction whenever any teen pushed the limits of their boundaries.

Jack is now an adult with his own home and a job that he loves. Unlike his siblings, he decided early on not to attend college. Even though it wasn't the path we saw for him, it was the path he wanted to follow, so we supported his decision. As a parent, I'm incredibly proud of him for having the courage to do it, and not the least bit surprised that he has found success.

I've since learned that raising teens requires a lot of understanding, and more importantly, open communication without judgment. By offering my son safe and productive ways to express his individuality (along with a little wiggle room to exert his independence), I've given him the greatest gift of all: self-confidence. Even though being a parent of four teens was a daunting task at times, it was not without reward.

Jack is proof that a daily dose of love and appreciation goes a long way in shaping a child's heart, and with it, an abundance of patience to survive the tumultuous teen years...along with an endless supply of hair dye.

Lessons from My Tween Son

Katie Smith

"I thought having three toddlers at the same time was hard, then they turned into teenagers" ~Katie Bingham Smith, Writer

I have two sons. One is very much like me; he looks like me, he can be anxious like me, he even twists his hair when he is in deep thought like I do. Because it is so obvious we are cut from the same cloth, our personalities have been known to clash.

My youngest son, Jack is a little different. He is the most laid back pre-teen I've ever known. He doesn't care about what goes on his body so long as he is comfortable. He is always is a fabulous mood, ready to entertain. The kid wakes up happy every single day. Jack is always a fun time.

He has taught me life is all about how you look at things. If you decide to be in a good mood, you will be, even if you don't suck back a jug of caffeine.

He has been in my life for twelve years, well, almost thirteen if you count my pregnancy, which of course counts. He was the biggest surprise I've ever had in my life. When I began to realize there may be a small chance I could be pregnant, the first two pregnancy tests I took were negative. He kept me guessing, or should I say questioning my sanity? I knew something was going on with my body despite those damn tests.

He came into my world showing me sometimes you are given a tremendous gift that will change your world even if you didn't know you wanted it. Also, you can't always count on a something to be ninety-nine percent accurate, even if it says so on the box. He was a trickster from the start.

When I was pregnant with him I gained so much weight my doctor decided it was best if I stopped getting weighed for every appointment. I craved peanut butter cups, cheeseburgers and crackers dipped in cream cheese. I had been a healthy eater since my teens and usually didn't eat like this on the regular until he started his journey in my belly. I couldn't stop my cravings if I wanted to. I was insatiable and didn't care at all about the rate my body was expanding.

He taught me in live in the moment and that I had mad eating skills which including eating a whole bag of chips in under forty minutes, something him and I now do together while watching Chopped on a random Wednesday night. Sometimes life is prepping you to make delicious memories for your future and you don't even know it.

 He doesn't care about material things unless you can fill them with water and throw them at people or make them explode. He has made sculptures out of paper clips and cares more about growing plants than he does about having a "cool" pair of shoes.

He has taught me there is never a reason to be bored, you can make anything from the junk drawer if you put your mind to it and listening to your kids laugh while having a water balloon must be what heaven is like.

Jack is a giver. This has nothing to do with how I have raised him although I would like to take all the credit, he has a knack for knowing when someone needs help, needs a hug, or just wants to biggest cookie. He is always happy to oblige. He doesn't even do it to get praise or to make himself feel better, he just believes it's what we all do.

He has taught me doing the right thing should be a habit. You should help others because it's the right way to live, not because

Tiffany O'Connor

you want attention or credit.

I walked into his room one afternoon and noticed a vase of dying dandelions he had on his dresser. I told him we should probably throw them out because it looked like they were dying. He said, "No mama, they aren't dying they are turning into wishes."

This boy, my son, has taught me there is so much magic in everything around us, sometimes you just have to look at life in a different way to find it.

My Battle Call
Valli Gideons

"A Message to My Teenager: Be kind. Wear deodorant. Pray. Talk more, Text less. Wash your PE clothes. Dance. Be quiet during the National Anthem. Brush your teeth. Read. Use please and thank you. Be gritty. Play outside. Unplug. Look up. Be still. Find your people. BE YOU!" ~My Battle Call

"Mom, tell me what it was like when I was born."

You were due on Thanksgiving Day. Only, you made us wait till the following Monday before you decided to enter the world. At least it got me out of cooking. But, boy it was a long road leading up to that day.

When the stick turned blue, your dad and I were overcome with joy. Only a few months prior, we had lost our first pregnancy at just twelve-weeks; we were elated to know we would be blessed with another baby. Within days of finding out we were pregnant again, an early ultrasound taught us about things like a ruptured corpus luteum and the lack of progesterone. Our doctor told us she thought we could save this pregnancy; we saw no other option but to fight. This meant inner-muscular injections daily for the first trimester.

Yes-when I say you can be a pain in the butt…it literally started before you were born. It seemed like a small price to pay to give you a chance at life.

And in true Battle fashion, you beat the odds by continuing to grow and thieve. When we made it past the twelfth week, we could finally take a deep breath and celebrate your impending arrival. You loved to hang out near my ribs and rocking and rolling was your favorite pastime. I craved peanut butter frozen yogurt, but that wasn't easily found in Cleveland. I settled for Taco Bell quesadillas and milkshakes. I taught spin class up until a week before my due date and my class made a habit out of making fun of my big belly.

The day finally arrived.

Labor lasted fourteen long hours. I guess that's why they say women who give birth experience amnesia. Because what I do remember is labor was harder than any long-distance triathlon or marathon I've ever done. I'm pretty sure your sister wouldn't be here if I truly recalled the whole thing. Dad was super helpful from start to finish-holding my hand, feeding me ice chips, and encouraging me. I didn't say more than a few words. Grandma was by my side. I later found out that in between contractions your Dad was watching Monday night football...I think the Packers won the game.

When I heard your first scream, I was literally just thankful you made it through the birthing process. It's funny how much I worried about you before you ever took your first breath outside of the womb.

You were surrounded by so many people who cared deeply for you. It was then I knew that you would have an abundance of love in your life. After the excitement of it all, when you failed the infant hearing screening, I wasn't even worried. I guess everything leading up to your birth just trumped the slim possibility it would be anything but fluid in your ears causing you to fail the routine test.

For two weeks straight Dad and I just tried to figure out how to care for you. It isn't easy being responsible for a newborn. You were a huge eater and you loved your burb cloth being placed near your chin (Aunt Vicki taught us that trick) You were not a fan of the expensive swing we bought for you; instead you loved sleeping nuzzled on Dad's chest.

When we loaded you into your infant car seat for the follow-up hearing test on that cold Cleveland morning, there was nothing but a small sliver in the deepest crevice of my core that imagined you would fail.

But that's the thing. As parents, you just don't know. The cards are held by something much bigger than what you are capable of imagining. There is a plan much more complicated than you can envision. The news of your severe to profound hearing loss started the next chapter of the journey. We indeed were in a fog for the days that followed trying to process it all.

After the shock of the diagnosis, the only option was to get to work. First, by accepting it and then by fighting to give you all the opportunities you deserved. You think I worry now? I am not going to sugarcoat it. The uncertainty for a new mom with a baby who was hard of hearing was plentiful. And, at times it felt like I wasn't cut out for this.

But as you stand here preparing to celebrate your fourteenth birthday, I know wholeheartedly I all was perfectly designed. You have always looked to the planets and stars and reached for them.

While in the early days we wondered…

Would you learn to talk?

You not only learned how to listen and develop speech and language, but you are also a motor mouth.

Would you be mainstreamed?

The further down this road we got, the more I realized "mainstream" wasn't important. Being included and accepted was everything. If you want to know what a mama bear looks like protecting her cubs, just watch a mother walking into an IEP meeting. It's pretty much the same...only the bear might be gentler.

Would you play sports?

To think there was a time we didn't think you would ever pick up a ball. Now I watch you on the football field and the track as you compete with an engine that never quits. Your athleticism is admirable because you have worked so hard to achieve it. It wasn't natural. It wasn't easy. But you never really have taken the easy route.

Would you make friends?

It turns out you are slow to warm up, even sometimes perceived as aloof. You lean into the people you call friends. Being the life of the party is not your style. I find your shy, awkwardness endearing.

Sure... you also exhibit all the other typical teenage things too. Your body odor is horrible. You sometimes forget to flush. Acne creams and tooth-paste scum line your bathroom countertop. Video games are king. You choose to sleep-in at the most inopportune times. Your breath stinks and you interrupt. You sometimes say and do dumb things. Mostly you reply to our life-lesson lectures with one-word answers and grunt-like noises.

It's the sum of all these things that have helped you develop a work ethic and unique tenacity. Besides your kind heart, your grit is what I know will take you far. Perhaps starting your life off having this battle gave you a unique view. Your perspective has shaped your lens; you see life with an empathetic heart and have the instinct to root for the underdog. *Unless the Steelers are losing. Because that quickly turns you into a fair-weather fan.

While a lot of parents are dreading these teen years, I am entirely in awe of them. Maybe because you have exceeded every expectation we had for you as a tiny baby bundled and strapped in his car seat leaving the hospital with a diagnosis of hearing loss. The truth is-I can't imagine you any other way. Most of my worry has lessened, and I am left with optimism and hope.

I am proud of you son. Being your advocate has been the greatest honor of my life. What I didn't know all those years ago is what being your momma would teach me about strength, resiliency, and love. The deepest kind of love you can only imagine in your wildest dreams.

You are and always will be my Battle call.

A Miracle at the County Fair
Jodie Utter

"I don't need to be a millionaire or have a perfect life, I just need to hear my child laugh." ~Utter Imperfection

When the auctioneer at the county fair brought his gavel down with a loud crack and hollered, "Sold! For fifty dollars per pound!" I flat out lost it. Overwhelmed in the best of ways and leaking tears like a fire hose, I stepped away from the fray for a moment to catch my breath and to process what had just happened to our daughter. To our whole family, really.

Weeks earlier, our daughter's market hog had succumbed to a fluke, unidentifiable illness and had to be put down. Unable to bring the hog to sale, she entered the auction ring that day with her backup feeder hog. He wasn't very fetching. He was a second chance. A Hail Mary. A stab at a last hurrah. He would have to do.

All afternoon, hogs had been selling for around nine dollars per pound, on average. Our girl needed to earn ten dollars per pound to break even on her expenses, which were heavily laden with vet bills from the prior months. Bringing in ten dollars per pound would've allowed her to avoid a loss but would also have kissed any profit goodbye. A profit on months of hard work is the very why kids take animals to fair for auction.

A second fiddle hog wasn't the only thing she brought into the auction ring that day. She also brought some heavy family baggage we'd all been carrying around for months. The year prior, in a breath-taking fall from grace, my husband had been forced out of his twenty-year career after a brief, consensual, and long since over affair with a co-worker had been discovered and reported to his superior. For several years, our kids and I knew nothing of his affair, as after he'd ended it he was replete with remorse and regret and had silently recommitted to our family and being the man he wanted to be for us.

In a sickening and nefarious turn of events, the story of his affair was hand-fed to our local media and became a top story for days on the radio, TV news, social media, and in the newspaper. My husband finally confessed his transgression to me just before the onslaught of media coverage began because he didn't want me to find out via the five o'clock news. Together, we then broke the disheartening news to our two teenagers, before someone else could.

Had we the choice, we likely never would've disclosed to our children the damaging details of their dad's unfaithfulness to me. When I tell you it was excruciating to have had to do so, I can only hint at just how gut twisting it was to admit a marital failure of epic proportions that an affair is to your kids.
I wanted to waste away and die in that moment rather than be living it. I'll never forget the overwhelming commingled urges I had to scream in rage, cry in misery, throw up, and physically hurt my husband over having to confide to our kids what he'd done. The horrible choice he'd made to set me aside in favor of another woman wasn't something we could protect them from, and I likely would have done just that forever if I could have.

After my husband's disclosure, my immediate and unwavering inclinations were to stay with him, keep our family intact, and try to rebuild our marriage. I can't explain my reaction and how quickly I came to it beyond the facts that I still loved him and he still loved me. When there are even vapory dregs of love left between two people, anything is possible. Without that love though, not so much. Owing to our still present mutual love and my husband's complete remorse for and ownership of his mistake, we were able to begin the hard work of rebuilding our marriage.

Tiffany O'Connor

No part of the restoration of our marriage was easy. Not the sleepless nights and deep hurt, not the months of couples therapy, not the loss of trust, and especially not helping our kids through the dueling very public and extremely personal calamity of it all. It would take a village, some angels, and a county fair to help get us all through it, only I didn't yet know it.

There are times in life when you'll find out who your friends truly are, and this was one of those times for us. At the onset of the grotesque public quality of our story, I remember realizing we were going to lose some friends over it. At first, the thought filled me with panic and a sense of paralyzing sadness. However, about six minutes later, I thought to myself, "Then bring it; show me who you are, people. I'm very interested to see who sticks around for us and who doesn't."

We did indeed lose a few friends. As we watched them pull back and push away, we were amazed at how relieved we were to see them go. For they weren't the real deal, never had been, and we were lucky to be realizing it. They were easy to let go of. In part, because they'd let go of us, but also because we saw the departures coming. What we didn't see coming was the arrival of new friends or the strengthening and solidifying of many of our existing friendships in the middle of our ordeal and attempt to heal. Not just in spite of our public troubles and trauma, but rather because of them.

We weren't prepared for how fiercely our true friends rallied around our family. Nor were we primed for brand spanking new friends aligning with us and doing the same. Our kids came home from school or from being out and about in our community to tell us how a coach or teacher or friend of ours had approached them—offering verbal support and encouragement to our entire family. They had people tell them what a great man they thought their dad to be, even though he'd made a grave mistake. Our children continually had people hovering around them and waiting in the wings to lift, support, and help them through their pain in a multitude of ways.

The phenomenon of having friends—both silver and gold—look right past my husband's flaws and missteps and focus instead on the bullseye of his core character and spotless record of twenty years in law enforcement, spent steadfastly serving our community, was jaw-dropping goodness. It was sustenance to our souls that balanced the scales of judgment and helped speed healing from his fall for us all. To have had people voice and demonstrate loyalty and compassion and offer a helping hand to our kids was grace upon grace and mercy upon mercy. Their kindness felt like warm shawls upon our shoulders and we'll forever be grateful for the comfort they provided.

Then we went to the county fair. Our daughter stepped into the auction ring with her second-string, benchwarmer hog and hit a home run when several of our friends began to bid on it, prompting a bidding war the likes of which we'd never seen. Unbeknownst to our family and either of them at the time, two different friends intended to purchase her hog that day and brought with them a 'whatever it takes' mentality to do so. What it took was fifty dollars per pound, and absolutely nobody saw that coming.

Our daughter's sale at the county fair was a reversal of fortunes for our family—quite literally and beautifully figuratively, as well. Her incredible sale was affirmation from our community of friends that they had our backs and weren't afraid to show it. It was confirmation they believed in us, in her, and in our collective worth as family at a time we struggled to believe in ourselves. It was high-level endorsement at a time we wrestled with concluding we deserved it. And that's the kind of sponsorship that counts the most.

It's easy to love others when they're shiny, happy people and when they do no wrong. When everything is coming up roses for them, and the world is their oyster. When people hit the skids though, from taking a wrong turn in life, and others still support them and work to help them get back on track—those folks should deem themselves angels sent from heaven. For that's precisely what they are.

There were angels among us that day at the county fair. And if it weren't for the hard parts of our story and the struggles we'd faced both as a family and individually, we'd never have been shown legendary levels of grace and kindness via this over-the-top generous deed for our daughter.

It takes a village, some angels, and something like a county fair to help us raise our kids up and through this so hard but still so worth it life. I'm so very blessed to have learned this firsthand.

This Is What Life with a Teenage Daughter Is Sometimes Like

Elizabeth Spencer

"What to expect when you're parenting a teenager. Expect to want to hold on. Expect to need to let go. Expect to celebrate. Expect to laugh, cry, worry, and wait. Expect to blame a lot on the hormones. Expect to be stretched. Expect to be inspired. Expect to love." ~Guilty Chocoholic Mama

I am the mom of two daughters and no sons. And when you are the mom of daughters and no sons, you hear three things pretty reliably when they are little:

#1: "They're adorable."

#2: "Are you going to try for a boy?"

#3: "Just wait until they get to be teenagers."

To #1, I usually replied, "Thank you."
To #2, I usually replied, "No, actually, we're going to try for a goldfish."

In response to #3, I usually just smiled and nodded as if I knew all about what I was waiting for when my adorable daughters got to be teenagers. Meanwhile, my brain was frantically whipping up all the possibilities of what life with teenage daughters might actually be like.

Well, now those adorable little girls are teenagers, so I know what life with them is like... at least in our house... at least some of the time.

Sometimes, life with a teenager daughter (TD) is like looking at a younger version of yourself who is at the same time her own amazing person.

Sometimes, life with a teenage daughter is like being in one room of the house with one family member while your TD is in another room. Your TD says something, and you and the other family member look at other in silent reaction to what she just said. From the other room, TD shouts, "I can hear you two looking at each other about me!"

Sometimes, life with a teenage daughter is like blaming the hormones. (Actually, life with a teenage daughter is often like blaming the hormones.)

Sometimes, life with a teenage daughter is like driving your TD to school and having her be in a happy, chatty mood. And then, with no warning, as if a switch has been flipped, she is suddenly, clearly upset about something. But when you ask if she's okay, she tells you "I'm just tired"—in as clipped a tone as it is possible to affect. And when, after a few minutes, you ask if something happened, she tells you, "I just don't feel good." (See "clipped tone.") So you tell her you love her and drop her off at school . . . and arrive home to this text: "Sorry, not really sure what that weird mood swing was about except that I didn't like my hair, but I just fixed that and I feel okay. Love you!" At which point you realize for the hundredth time that emotional whiplash is a THING when you are parenting a teenage girl but that when it whips back in the direction of honesty and transparency and trust and love, it's worth every bump in the wild ride.

Sometimes, life with a teenage daughter is like parenting someone who might one day become your best friend.

Sometimes, life with a teenage daughter is like overhearing the following conversation: "I'm mad at you!" "Well, I'm mad at you for being mad at me." (At least everything balanced out.)

Sometimes, life with a teenage daughter is like looking at a shirt on the clearance rack when you're out shopping together and wondering if you like it and having your TD come out of the dressing room and tell you, "No, mom, you don't like that." So at least then you know.

Sometimes, like with a teenage daughter is not saying what you want to say.
Sometimes, life with a teenage daughter is like having one daughter working on her hair at one mirror in the house and coming to the door of the bathroom where TD is working on her hair and asking, "Well, what do you think?" And you, the innocent bystander, wait with bated breath for TD to render her opinion and then breathe a sigh of relief when she exclaims, "That's what celebrities' hair looks like! It's so pretty!" And life, mercifully, carries on.

Sometimes, life with a teenage daughter is like seeing the beauty in her that she cannot see in herself but trying with all the power of love to help her to see it.
Sometimes, life with a teenage daughter is like never being quite sure what version of your girl will emerge from her room on any given morning.

Sometimes, life with a teenage daughter is like owning 7,000 bobby pins but not being able to lay your hands on A SINGLE ONE when you actually need it.

And sometimes, life with a teenage daughter is like looking at your daughter and remembering how, the first time you saw her, you thought you could not possibly love her more than you did at that moment but realizing that you were wrong about that because you do. And you also realize that this is one of the best things you've ever been wrong about in your entire life.

My Best Parenting Advice: Buy Post-it Notes

Jelise Ballon

"She frustrates me beyond words and makes my heart swell with pride and joy. She has a knack for shutting me out while sitting directly beside me, and for being more in tune to my feelings than anyone else, knowing precisely the right moment to give me a giant hug in the middle of the kitchen at the end of a horribly long day." ~Neither Height nor Depth

If you are parenting teenagers, my advice to you is to buy Post-it Notes. Lots and lots of Post-it Notes.

I have three teenagers, and that means a lot of juggling schedules -- sports schedules, school schedules, dance recital schedules, orthodontist appointments, after-school job schedules, volunteer schedules, etc. As mom, I am the master schedule keeper. Everything gets written down in my calendar, and then I shout out reminders like I'm Siri reading off everyone's iCal notifications. All the people in my house rely on me and my calendar. We're in a committed relationship and, together, we basically keep this family moving like a well-oiled rusty old machine.

The problem, however, is that I don't do mornings, which is prime time for daily reminders. My husband, God love him, does the morning routine four days per week and gets the kids off to school so I can sleep in a bit (I know, I'm very lucky, but to be fair, he's slept through every nighttime stomach bug and bad dream emergency for the last sixteen years, so I figure it balances in the end). His approach to mornings is a bit different from mine. As long as everyone is out the door mostly dressed with some kind of bag in their hand by 7:45-ish, he's good. And hey, when you're running the show, you do it your way.

My approach, the one morning a week I'm in charge, is more like a pre-flight check on the Shuttle Atlantis with me shouting from my bathroom things like: "don't forget to feed the cats!", "You have basketball today, make sure you packed your shorts," "we're leaving in fifteen minutes, so you better be putting on socks and shoes right now!", "did you get your History homework off the printer?", "why is it taking you ten minutes to put on one shoe?!?", "yes, you have to eat breakfast.", "no, you cannot wear shorts and a t-shirt in twenty-degree weather.", "For the love of Lady Footlocker, PUT ON YOUR SHOES ALREADY!!"

OK, so that last one about the shoes? I've been shouting that one from my bathroom since 2003. Some things never change.

On the days I know I'll be sleeping through the next morning's madness, I go through my list of reminders the night before – partly because I worry about who is going to forget what, and partly because if I don't I'll lay awake all night imagining scenarios of three grumpy and hormonal humans walking through the door at 6 p.m. telling me how it was the "worst day ever" because they forgot their soccer cleats and had to practice in their fake UGGs. While I verbally remind my darlings of all they have the next day, encouraging them to get everything they need ready and packed the night before, even suggesting they *gasp* write some of this down themselves, by 10 p.m. no one even cares anymore and there's a 50% chance two out of three kids have passed out fully dressed with the lights still on in their bedroom.

This is where the Post-it Notes come in. Knowing the morning will be a mess and I'll be tucked under my covers dreaming of pedicures and a cell phone bill that is less than $150, I write my three muffins little Post-it love notes like these:

"Olivia, Here's $10 for lunch. I expect at least $2 in change back from this. Love, mom"

"Hannah, please unload the dishwasher before you leave for school, unless you'd like me to change your Instagram profile pic to that picture of you when you were three and smeared Vaseline all over your hair. Love, mom"

"Daniel, for all that is good and decent in this world, please don't forget to put on deodorant before you leave! Love, mom"

Because if you give a thirteen year old $9.89 for lunch, she will spend $9.90. Because, sixteen-year-olds still forget to do their daily chore, even when it's been their *daily* chore for FOUR YEARS. Because middle school boys think deodorant is unnecessary, and making their mother gasp for air when they hug her is funny.
Because kids.

So my advice to you parents embarking on the teen years is this;

1. Invest in Post-it Notes,

2. Hang on to that sense of humor, you're going to need it,

3. Always sign "love, mom" or "love, dad." Your kids will have stopped reading by that point, but it will feel less like nagging and more like a daily affirmation.

Baby, You Can Drive My Car
Jennifer Hurvitz

"My mom used to say, "when your boys (teens) are acting the worst is when the need you the most."...dammit, she was right. Not only is it when they need me the most, it's when they want me the most. They just never, ever admit it." ~ Jennifer Hurvitz, Author

I knew the day was coming. I tried to brace myself. I even upped my meds. Ha.

But honestly, there is nothing that prepares you for the sheer horror you feel the very first time you drive in a motorized vehicle….With your teenager.

Nada.

I know you're reading this and nodding your head in agreeance. Some of you are laughing or giving me a "hell yes!" But it is the truth! Nothing can ever completely equip you for sitting shotgun while your fifteen-year-old man-child is behind the wheel controlling that vehicle instead of you. NOTHING. You can chuckle while you listen to all the surreal stories, about your friend's kids smashing into mailboxes or killing squirrels, sure. And it's always thoughtful when they remind you to increase your insurance policy on your vehicles. Oh, and how cute is it when you get that magnet made for the back of YOUR car that says, "STUDENT DRIVER." And thank you to all of you who still act like idiots when you see that magnet! Just wait until YOUR kid is a teenager! Yeesh. But yes, everything is unrivaled when the teen sitting behind that wheel is yours. Different when you hand over YOUR keys, and he is now calling all the shots; you can't do a damn thing about it...

Helpless and vulnerable.

Unable to do anything but sit next to him and talk him through it.

I'll never forget that very first morning...

We checked the mirrors, adjusted the seat, and rechecked them. Then we checked the mirrors again. Oh, and then the seat. And then we changed the mirrors. Ok!! We are good, babe! We cross-checked and rechecked, and then we decided that it was finally time to back out of the driveway. So we did. He looked down at the screen (which we didn't even have back in the day I chose to remind him for the ten thousandth time), and it beeped to tell him a car was coming.

He stopped.

Abruptly. But hey, at least he stopped. The vehicle passed behind us, and he continued down the driveway onto the street. I told him he was doing a great job! Positive reinforcement is the key...Got to keep it light and positive. Yes! His younger brother was in the back seat, laughing. I wanted to kick his butt but decided there were a time and a place, and this was neither. I continued to praise Jonah," Excellent work, honey." And as we approached the main road, I noticed my armpits were starting to sweat a bit. Do you think he saw? I genuinely hope not, because that would have hurt his feelings at the time. He would've thought I was nervous. Ha! I bent my head down to take a look under my pits...and then I realized what I was doing (taking MY eyes off the road) I popped my head up....

Just in time to see him pull out into oncoming traffic...ummm. HELLLLOO????

Jonah kept on driving, ignoring the big, red STOP sign.

He didn't slow down or stop.

He just turned right into the traffic, and honestly, I think he thought he could just speed up really, really fast and the massive truck on his ass would just slow down? Well, it was obviously too late for me to scream STOP which is what I should have done BEFORE he pulled out onto the road...but now, we were literally on the road, so screaming "STOP" would have been well, ummm... really, really bad! So instead, I did what any sane mother would do,

I screamed, **"DRIVE FUCKING FASTER, JONAH OR WE ARE GOING TO DIE!"**

So he did, he drove faster.

He floored it and slammed his foot all the way to the floor. He went from about twenty-five to sixty in like thirty seconds flat. I was full-on sweating, and his brother was laughing so hard I thought he was going to piss his pants. Jonah started to calm down when he saw the truck was back off in the distance. He took a few deep breaths and slowed down...I began to giggle; he did too. Then we looked at each other and laughed.

My bad; but we were all alive...and he totally recovered.
Just as I started to calm down, I heard Zac laughing from the back seat, and then I listened and heard my voice and me screaming! OMG, that little shit had recorded the entire thing? Yes! Zac seemed to think that this near-death-scenario was all so amusing that it should be recorded for his Snap Chat and Instagram accounts. Well, Jonah was pissed, and he started screaming from the front, that he was. "Going to kill Zac". I immediately tried to diffuse the situation. I turned around and went to rip the phone from Zac's hands even though I knew it was way more important to stay calm while Jonah was driving! Zac jumped out of my way, and as I reached over to try one more time, I noticed Jonah

was blinking furiously. Like there was something in his eyes! This really couldn't get any worse! But....we were almost at the Starbucks this was the trip from hell!

It's was the sun. The sun?

Without hesitation, I reached up and pulled down the visor right in front of this face. What? I thought I was helping! He couldn't see a damn thing! He flipped it back up while swerving into the lane next to him, "Jennifer! You can't do that while I'm driving! Where are my sunglasses?" Oh, and for the record, he is only allowed to call me by my first name while he is driving. And why do you ask? Because it's the only time, I can't beat his ass! So I gave him a look of death and pulled his glasses out of the glove box. Against my better judgment, I handed them to him. I watched him nervously as he attempted to put them on with one hand while driving with the other.

I wanted to puke. I tried so hard not to help him; I sat on my hands. I knew he could do it; he is fifteen for the love of God! He's not a baby. Ugh. He put them on, and he could see again. Problem diverted, and I was sweating so badly at that point, I needed a new tee shirt. Even between my boobs were sweaty. TMI?

And of course, Zac was dying in the back seat.

Just you wait until next year when it's your turn, I screamed at him.

Then, I saw it. Our final destination was quickly approaching.

Now, I'm sure you can all relate to this exact scenario. Feeling so out of control? Trying so hard to stay calm, while your baby is entirely in charge of a "weapon" made from a ton of steel. And he's doing one hell of a job! But just as I was about to give him props...he tried to get all Mr. Over Achiever and change the song on the radio! Oh, hell no, my friend. Focus, I told him. There is no need to worry about the songs on the radio! You can drive in silence, and we can chit-chat! Put your hands on that wheel at ten and two...don't get all crazy on me. I'm so sure, he wanted music? Concentrate on the road, mister. I don't even think he knows how to get from our house to school for the love of God! He's been texting while I've been driving for the last five years! Do you know I have a girlfriend that got a call from her daughter the day she got her license from the gas station? She was LOST on her way to the nail salon that they had been going to for the past six years together!

Oh please make this stop.

I was breathing. Just breathe, Jennifer. I told him to slow down we were coming up to the Starbucks, and we needed to turn right into the parking lot. Ummm, honey, we needed to slow down-....dear, forty-five will not do. Breathing. I said it one last time as I reached for the door handle with the grip of death and started to pump the fake break on my side of the car. I began seeing all kinds of horrible images in my head: us hitting the median, the car flipping, and I started to panic!

He was breaking...but not soon enough. Thirty miles per hour...no!

JONAH SAM SLOW THIS CAR DOWN!!!!

He turned the car into the parking lot going twenty miles per hour, and it was undoubtedly on two wheels. Zac was laughing, I was shrieking, and Jonah was utterly calm....as he pulled the car into a spot between a Range Rover and a beat up Toyota in the Starbucks parking lot.

He shut off the engine, looked over at me and said with a little smirk, "Well, Jen that was pretty close to perfect for my first time behind the wheel, wouldn't you say?" He then jingled the keys in front of me, and as I reached out my shaky hand, to grab them, I said," You can call me MOM now, my sweet boy. We are no longer moving, and I'll be driving home."

"Oh, and we need to work on your turns!" I giggled.

I reached over and tousled his hair, thinking how could it even be possible that the baby that once sat in a car seat facing backward was now driving this car? Taking a big sigh and holding back my tears...I got out of the car. Thankfully, I planted both of my feet on solid ground. I walked over and hugged him tightly. I love that he still lets me hug him in public; one day he won't. But I secretly hope he always will.

As I watched my boys walk into Starbucks, I realized how quickly time passes. How fast they grow up and how I only have a few more years with them until they go off to college. Ugh, I'm crying as I write this, Y'all. And honestly, as scary as this driving thing is, I would do it again and again....just to be in the seat next to them.

I call shotgun! Every single time. ;)

For Jonah and Zac my two favorite teenagers

The Teen Years – Does All This Sitting Make My Butt Look Big?

Heather LeRoss

"Some days, my teens amaze me with their maturity, empathy for others, and sweet hugs. Other days I'm wondering why there's only one pair of underwear in the weekly laundry and yelling, "It only takes one finger to flush!" It's never boring." ~Tipsy Tiaras

Fifteen years ago, when I had my son, it was hard for me even to envision a time where he was a teenager. I tried, but most times, I remember thinking, "I can't even imagine him being five!" Five came and went, and with each passing year, I would marvel, "Oh my gosh, I can't believe I have a six, seven, eight-year-old!" When I'd try to imagine him as a teen, I was at a loss. I knew what to expect from the teen years; angst, hormones, moodiness, disengagement, eye rolls, smells (ok, seriously, what is WITH the smells??), but what I didn't anticipate was ME; how I would be.

Here I sit now with a teenage son, and I'm finding myself plagued with a general feeling of unease. Not because the teen years are harder than I thought, in many ways, they're much easier. I actually like my teen. I love talking with him, hearing how he thinks about things and views the world. We talk a lot, and for that I'm grateful. He has a wicked sense of humor, and I love seeing him laugh. I don't care for his musical tastes, and his hygiene leaves a little to be desired, but I truly adore who he is as a young man.

This feeling of unease comes because no one told me that the teen years would have me sitting so much. Not literally, but my life right now seems to be about me sitting in the messy middle. I'm busier now than I've ever been with lots to do – a lot of my doing seems to be driving, and I'm not idle, but if you asked me what life is all about right now, I'd say sitting and waiting.

Sitting, waiting in the messy middle of my life where it feels like everything is on pause, waiting for the "next big thing" to happen. With my oldest sixteen is looming large, along with driving, first job, first love, first heartbreak - so many firsts to come. My youngest is ten, not yet a teen, but I see the signs. Like recently, his reluctance to wear the cool new Pokémon swim shirt I bought him. His eyes lit up when I first showed it to him, his smile settling into my heart as I heard the whisper, "Good job Momma. You made your boy happy." Until we got ready to go to the pool and he insisted on wearing the swim shirt inside out, so the Pokémon symbol was hidden. Sob. The self-awareness is happening with him, the comparisons to other kids, and the insecurity. Seeing his innocence and obliviousness to what others think start to fade replaced by judgment and wariness has bent me some, made my shoulders slump, and my heart heavier because I remember my teen years, and I know what's to come.

But right now, it's a soft pause. It's this middle stage with my boys between the sweet, innocent young boys I've known and loved, and this grown-up stage of young men who I have yet to get to know. It's knowing that there are scary, heartbreaking, joyous, exciting things ahead, but they're all ahead of me.

It's this stage in life where raising teens means everything has progressed. It's not just my boys who've gotten older; my parents have aged. Time is starting to make things harder for them, bending them too, slowing them down. I know what's coming although it's too scary to write. Right now, it's just a whisper of what's to come, but I know someday – sooner than I want – it will be a scream in my life. A howling of loss, fear, sadness, and regrets. I'm combating this knowledge with calling more, seeking out ways to spend more time together, thanking the universe for giving me one more year, one more day.

The messy middle includes watching my friendships wither. I'm losing connections to my tribe, some women who've been with me since before my kids were even a dream. On the one hand, some of the relationships weren't healthy, I can acknowledge this, but it's still hard. I know a new tribe is out there, but again, I'm sitting here waiting. Waiting to find my people, my women who will champion my dreams, gently hold my secrets and fears, who will lift me up when I'm bent, helping me to see ahead of me. Women who will do this all with the most gracious of love, the kindest of words, and the best hugs. Once I find these women and believe me, I'm looking, putting myself out into the "friendship dating pool" which in some ways is harder than the regular dating pool, I'll return this love and kindness ten-fold, grateful for their presence, support, and trust. I'll also bake them the best treats known to man because I like to put my love into the food I make. They'll taste my devotion with cinnamon and sugar.

Time isn't stopping for me in this whole aging process either. While I want to scream the cliché, "But I don't FEEL forty-three!!!" there are reminders of aging every day for me now. From having a hysterectomy last year and removing the parts of my body that grew my boys, the parts that kept them safe while I nurtured them into existence, to the other "mom-cliché" of having to cross my legs when I sneeze and avoid jumping on trampolines (also coughing, laughing too hard, running, etc.) time is changing me too. My hips ache, I have on on-going battle with the nerves in my neck and back which recently seized up on me while I was ... wait for it ... pounding my chicken for dinner one night. The pain was so intense and kept me down for a few days, so I've since decided my husband will be the one in charge of beating the meat. Haha, see what I did there? I inserted a dirty joke.

Which leaves me with how I cope these days with all the change and change to come – humor, writing, reading, and lots of therapy. Finding things to laugh at (usually me - tripping, saying the most awkward of things to a stranger, or finding blueberries in my teeth after a day spent out and about), getting my feelings down on paper, escaping into someone else's story, and having a safe place to be the most honest and vulnerable version of me in front of someone who doesn't judge is a sanity saver. Also, I eat. I'm not saying everyone should eat their feelings but for me cooking, reading recipes sites, eating, thinking about what I'm going to eat and when the next food break is, helps with the sitting and waiting for the next big thing life is going to deliver.

I know there are a lot of "nexts," a lot of "firsts" coming, and a lot of unknowns. It may be the bliss of seeing my son fall in love for the first time; it may be celebrating another birthday with my parents, thankful I have the joy of their presence still. It might be another wedding anniversary with my husband, or it could simply be the next wonderful book I escape into. While I can't predict the future, there are some guarantees, and right now I'm choosing to sit and wait with the comfort of knowing that no matter what the next big thing is, it'll happen in a life that's filled with love, laughter, acceptance, and lots and lots of cake because cake soothes the savage beast...or something along those lines.

Building Trust with No Consequence Conversations

Shelby Spear

"Raising teens made me a better human. Thank you, the mystique of prayer, Goose over ice, and God's Grace." ~Finding Grace in the Mishmash

"We are taking you kids out to dinner tonight. Fancy place downtown, so dress nice."

This announcement to my three teens marked one giant leap for me and one giant leap for momkind on the dusty surface of childrearing. My husband and I planned a communal backdrop for what would be a magnanimous twist to our parenting repertoire.

"I'll have the strongest drink on the menu, please," I asked the waitress with a smile, hoping the urgency of my request didn't alarm the boppers. My hubby raised an eyebrow at me. I raised both of mine in return. Secret code for, "Why are you doing that?" and "Don't you bother asking!"

Seventeen. Fifteen. Thirteen. The ages of my offspring when the hubs and I decided to put into play a new technique we learned from the television show, *My Wife and Kids*. When beer labels and bliss chocolate foil messages aren't providing wisdom anymore, a parent of acne bearers becomes desperate.

"Learning how to parent from a pretend family in a sitcom isn't as drastic as it sounds," said no one ever. But when you have three kids living under your roof whose brains aren't fully developed, random is the new normal. Lest you think our newfound philosophy was pure willy-nilly, we also engaged in prayer asking God for affirmation of our plan. He gave us a green light.

While the kiddos scarfed down gazpacho, weird appetizers, and entrees a la fancy, I pushed food around my plate with a fork. My gut was in knots.

"Eh em. Your dad and I have something serious to discuss with you."

Smiles and laughter turned to blank faces, followed by my oldest smirking and cackling, "Let me guess, you're pregnant?"

"Hilarious, but no. We know how difficult these teenage years are with temptations, stresses, self-esteem, hormone frenzy, peer influences. Dad and I have always promised we will be available to you if you get in a bad situation with drinking or otherwise. We are expanding this recipe to include a new family policy regarding open communication: no consequence conversations.
We will hold random family meetings in which you are free to tell us anything you want—maybe a poor choice you made, the tough decision you're discerning, the predicament you're in, a temptation you're facing, etc. Whatever you reveal is immune from consequences. We are here to pray for you and offer guidance, support, and encouragement without judgment or reprimand."

Our table became center court at Wimbledon, the kids looking back and forth at one another. No doubt sending subliminal messages of shock and awe. Teens don't use eyebrow talk. That's an adult power.

Oldest: "So, what you're saying is no matter what we tell you, no punishment?"

Husband: "That's correct."

Middle:

Youngest:

The crickets coming from kid two and three were because our middle son is a thinker and probably still on sentence one of my bomb drop. Kid three, daughter innocent of all things, was already in mourning for what she knew was about to go down. Siblings know things about each other. She knew things about stuff we didn't even know things about; ergo her mourning for my mom soul.

Our oldest had already pushed the boundaries of tomfoolery, so my better half and I expected to hear something. But my inner mom was butting heads with my outer mom regarding my ability to refrain from getting angry, upset, or worse. Hence the public setting to convene our first run with such a conversation. I was hopeful a room full of strangers meant a tempered reaction.
Oldest: "Are the kids allowed to call a family meeting any time we want?"

Slick isn't he? He formulated a plan for manipulating the system in under a minute.

Me: "Why? So you can do whatever you want and then call a meeting? So you don't get in trouble?"

Oldest:

Bam. In less than ten seconds, his hackneyed attempt to dupe a supermom was put to shame.

Husband: "Go ahead, guys. Tell us anything you want. This is our first family meeting with no consequences."

Thus began a tumultuous season of unrest in my mom's heart. Our daughter had nothing to share, the oldest slung a few arrows, but the middle son cored me like an apple. He is our seventy-five degrees and breezy kid: soft spoken, gentle, kind, rarely argumentative, rule follower. His reveal stunned me. Not because the truth shared was atypical for a teen, more so because of my white glove perception of his behavior. A part of me never expected him to make a poor choice and to find out he did split my gala into wedges.

The fallout was unfortunate for my poor son. For a kid who used to cry when listening to the Carpenters, the mortal disappointment on my face broke his sensitive heart. I experienced a dark night of the soul that evening; bellowing into the universe from the shady side of the motherhood moon, "What did we just get ourselves into? Really, God? This was a good idea? Did you have your fingers crossed behind your back when you affirmed our decision to do this?"

Although I went to bed feeling the burden of everything the kids revealed, I woke up the next morning with a fresh perspective. God whispered a knowing into my spirit overnight, which said, you did the right thing. The fruits of our grueling labor would come. The harvest has been amazing. Since our first meeting seven years ago, all three of our children have opened their worlds to us, and I mean their WORLDS. For the sake of privacy and respect for my children, I harbor the details. The laundry list would make many moms lose their marbles and their lunch. But, the heartache, worry, anxiety, stress, and confusion for a parent has a beautiful flip side: choosing to be a sounding board for our children creates a safe respite for them to be vulnerable without veiling the truth. They aren't ashamed to confide because they trust us. Then we can be there when they need us.

Surrendering my kids to God is torturous at times, but I'll suffer any day over being unaware of my kid's struggles. Ignorance may be bliss…

But what if they are suffering in silence?

Living a lie?

Covering up a secret?

Contemplating horrific ways out of a mess?

As a mom, knowing what's going on provides an opportunity to guide and help find a solution. Sometimes we can only pray and love them. But having the chance to place my children's problems at the foot of the Cross so He can help them with their life is a privilege. In case you're wondering, our kids were still punished. Family rules and expectations didn't change. But we had a balance. When our teens felt they were in over their heads, we were there. Each has expressed heartfelt gratitude for the safe haven. God knew what he was doing. Since He talks through burning bushes and floating hands, there should be no surprise in him talking through Damon Wayans.

We listened to our kids.

We prayed.

We learned to Trust.

We survived.

Our family has grown stronger in faith and love as a result.

WE ARE BLESSED.

From Eye Rolls to Sleepovers, We're in this Together

Shannon Day

"One day you're the queen of the fucking castle and the next, you're hanging off the edge of motherhood's cliff with nothing but a partner less sock to cling to. This is what it feels like to parent through the teen years." ~ Martinis and Motherhood

When it comes to surviving the teen years, my advice is simple: Get out while you can! Tahiti, Japan, Hawaii, Milan…. pretty much anywhere will do. Just pack your bags and go.

GO!

Admit it, you're fantasizing about hopping on a plane right now, aren't you? But though tempting, we parents can't leave the country indefinitely due to eye roll overload and a surge of newly sprouted greys. We signed up for this parenthood gig, and we need to finish what we started. Not that the role of a parent ever actually ends…

And we thought the toddler years were tough. Ha ha ha ha. HAAAA ha ha ha ha ha haaaaaaa. Sigh.

So, since fleeing isn't an option will you do me a favor and promise to be there to hold each other? That's right; hold on to your fellow parents during these teen years. Literally or just figuratively. As in, hold out a glass of Pinot or be there to respond to (without judgment) a frustrated parenting text or to share in a simple (yet powerful) knowing glance that says: "I get it. I've been there. We can survive this."

We can survive the teen years, together.

Every single one of us is parenting our way blindly through the chaos, the sass, the bids for independence, the clashing of characters; we've got so much going on. If eye rolls translated to dollars, we'd be wealthy AF. Sadly, this is not the case. Luckily for us, though, when it comes to our teenagers there's some pretty cool stuff happening as well.

A part of me even feels excited for these upcoming years when I get to watch my eldest girl learn to spread her wings and hit the skies. Admittedly, there is another part of me that misses the days when the two of us would curl up together, inside her castle-shaped play tent, watching *Dora* and sipping pretend tea.

Whenever we used to ask our adorable little girl to do or to stop doing something, she'd say: "Okay Mum-may" (she was born in England, so that was my name back then). So easy going, she was; a joyful, mini side-kick who loved to skip her way from A to B. She even tossed in the occasional booty wiggle along the way for the entertainment of anyone who might be watching.

That former *Dora* wannabe is fourteen-years-old now, and with attitude and swagger, she is blazing the trail to Teenville with her little sisters (ages eight and ten) hot on her Sperry's. I can already see my eight-year-old is on the fast track there. That's right; our eldest daughter is no longer a cuddly, affable bundle of sweetness. She no longer skips from A to B, though she does the odd back tuck here and there. Nor does she shake her booty for the entertainment of strangers, though I imagine she does it for her friends when they're together.

She is now a teenaged-force to be reckoned with, complete with "on fleek" brows and an uncanny knack for seeing through other people's bullshit. She goes to tumbling competitions, and she takes on babysitting gigs to pay for her trips to Starbucks and the mall. She's a typical teen, with a hint of cynicism that comes across as wise one day and pure Instagram-induced pessimism the next.

She also has some pretty great friends. And, not surprisingly, she'd be with them 24-7 if she could. She's in that friend-centric stage of life. I remember it well. This also means that none of her plans include sipping tea or hanging out with me in a tent (not willingly, anyway). But there is one thing that she still likes to do every once in a while.

My girl still likes to have a sleepover with her mom sometimes. And last weekend, during one of our sleepovers, I was gifted a little bit of magic. My husband was away for work, which means the kids were taking turns sleeping on his side of the bed. They do this on a rotating basis whenever he's out of town. I'm a fan, I admit it. Last Saturday, it was my eldest daughter's turn. She and I had stayed up late watching *Sixteen Candles* together (such a classic).

I popped my head in to say goodnight to my middle girl, my little girl, and their friends (they too were having a sleepover). My big girl and I jumped into bed and soon found ourselves laughing; in total stitches over things that would, "literally," only be funny to us: silly voices, made-up words, weird faces. We were like two kids having our own sleepover; tears of laughter streamed down my cheeks. At one point, I had to run to the bathroom. I almost peed my pants.

IT WAS AWESOME!

But, it got even better when (mid-giggle) the bedroom door flung open. And there stood my middle daughter, hand on her hip like a miniature mom. She was NOT impressed.

"MOM!" She shouted. "We are TRYING to sleep. And you two are being TOO LOUD!"

I felt like I was a kid again, in trouble. I stifled an incoming snort-laugh.

"Are you… joking?" I asked.
"NO!" She said. "We can't sleep with all this laughing!"

"She isn't joking," said the voice of her little sleepover buddy. "We ARE trying to sleep."

And there it was. A moment so priceless, it was absolute magic!

"Sorry girls. We'll be quiet now," I said, trying to keep a straight face.

And we were quiet.

The door closed. My teenage daughter and I gave each other a knowing smile, snuck out one last giggle, and went to sleep. And that's the stuff! The stuff that makes the battles more bearable. The stuff that gives us hope and little moments of connection. It's the simple moments like these that we can cling to when the rapids get rough.

So, I guess my advice to parents aiming to survive the teen years is: Hang on tightly, mamas and papas. You will get through these teen years and the bullshittery that comes along with them. You'll be okay, and so will they.

Just remember to laugh whenever you can, appreciate the little moments of connection, and hold each other because we're in this together.

The Glorious Thing That Happens to Every Teen Mom

Christine Carter

"Six things your teen needs you to say: I hear you. I understand how you are feeling. I see so many gifts in you. I believe you. I love you, no matter what. I am always here for you." ~The Mom Cafe

I walked out onto the field searching for my boy, hoping he had found where he needed to be. This was the first day of his first job as a referee for the city's younger kids' soccer league. My son's been playing soccer since he was three and loves the sport, so when he learned of this referee employment opportunity, he was determined to get through the many hours of training to land this job.

Scanning several fields filled with little tykes swarming around balls and parents cheering them on, I finally found my boy.

And in that instant, something happened.

It's that glorious thing that happens to every teen mom. It can come during big events or hit you out of the blue. It is the culmination of so many years that in that split second, it all clicks and hits your heart hard.

Your eyes squint to focus in on your child while your throat closes and you choke back tears. It feels somewhat like a punch in the gut, but it comes from within...It's that sudden surge of profound emotion, realizing how much your kid has grown.

They start out so tiny, so fragile, and so new to life and all it will bring. The days are filled with constant caretaking in the blurry beginning, while you're just trying to survive. But the blurry days turn to blurry years and those blurry years transform our kids into grown human beings, and my gosh it can take our breath away.

On this particular day and in that instant, I compared these little kids to my big kid on that field, noticing the magnitude of the difference and how ironic it felt that my boy was now a referee instead of a little tyke chasing the ball and, well, that did it.

Or on another particular day, when my son was describing something mundane, so ordinary, but his voice sounded different, his tone and the shape of his words sounded more like a man.

You flash back to your baby in those early years and look before you to see the evidence of all those long days and sleepless nights, all the stages and phases you endured for too long or fretted would never come. And you are stunned, realizing every single detail of your job has brought your child to this moment, and my gosh, it's a glorious thing.

These moments are filled with astonishment. Like how on earth did THIS happen? Abruptly following this gasp is a massive revelation that time is running too fast and all you can see are fuzzy fragments of yesterdays, and you wish it all back, or at the very least, beg for tomorrow to slow down.

But then you realize the miracle unfolds with light-speed time, where your child is transforming right before your watery, aging eyes. It's the relentless evolving path we all venture down from the moment we give birth, and it's an incredible wonder, isn't it?

Yeah. It really is.

Motherhood can be a hard, thankless job. It is exhausting and often filled with tedious caretaking and endless teaching. It can spin us into a frenzied, frantic mess, and bring us to the break of defeat more than we care to admit. It's a profound journey indeed, full of our greatest joys and our deepest, darkest lows. And when the teen years hit, my gosh it gets so hard. You thought you were so busy with your little ones, you thought it was so hard and exhausting, and you thought your worries would lessen as they age, but you had no idea about this new level of busy, of exhaustion, of worry.

But these moments? The moments when we are caught off guard, stopped in our scurrying shuffling barely surviving tracks to notice the undeniable changes that are occurring in our kids, right before our tearing-tired eyes. The moments when we are suddenly immersed in the extraordinary joy of witnessing our child grow to become the person he or she was meant to be and the exhaustion lifts for just this moment and is filled with wonder, with awe.

There's something sacred about it. It's these profound moments that buoy us back up with new strength and stamina to carry on, to carry out this exhausting, maddening, miraculous mission we were given to raise our kids.

This is the glorious thing that reminds us just how incredible parenting can be.

Enough
Lisa Leshaw

"Never underestimate the power of a teen to love their Mama. It may come through in a series of grunts and grumbles, yet if you listen ever so carefully, it's love shaped by peer pressure." ~Lisa Leshaw, Writer

Half-way between his eye-roll and a mumble, I hugged my fifteen-year-old teenage son from behind while he leaned into the fridge for the tenth time in as many minutes.

"Ma, jeez, what are you DOING?"

I thought it was obvious. Then I realized this stranger before me didn't recall our squishy hugs and Eskimo nuzzles routine from an earlier prehistoric time. Until this year, they had been the norm. His and mine. The problem was that I recalled them with a yearning often too consuming to brush aside.

Enough that I'd already received the "don't stand outside the locker room when the game is over; I'll meet you at the car" lecture. I'd earned that spot. Water bottles in hand. High-fives at the ready. Warm words of encouragement when needed. Tons of cheering too. His teammates met me with their signature "Hey Mrs. L." each time, which probably signaled the start of my downfall.

Enough that when I pick him up after-school, I have to remain nonchalant and NEVER approach the building nor acknowledge him in front of his friends. He must have forgotten that only years earlier he craned his neck so hard to find my car in the pick-up line. When spotted, he'd barrel towards me with unbridled enthusiasm, waving his school assignment high above his little head, the gold star flapping in the breeze.

Enough that the "how was school today?" is no longer worthy of as much as a grunt.

Enough that the snack I set out every day for eleven years, beginning with the "Thomas the Train" plastic plate and matching place mat, is no longer requested. I'm informed that he'll grab a bite after practice with the team. One of the cool Dads will drive the kids to Applebee's and back. Excuse me; cool MOM over here. In case you haven't noticed.

Enough that I have to compete against two video games, a girlfriend, a cell phone, two football playoffs on the television, for a mere glimpse of his presence.

Enough that I miss everything about his littleness. I guess if I'm honest, I miss everything his littleness needed from me. I was once the center of his universe. Christopher Robin to his Winnie the Pooh. Snoopy to his Woodstock. Does he remember the Lucky Charm bridges we erected from cereal bowl to cereal bowl always ending in the pink hearts? Does he remember his little face smushed against the school bus window; his tears first then mine when the bus turned the corner? What about blanket fort Sundays? Scientific experiments to see if gummy bears float in the tub? Thumbs that tasted yucky? Bogeymen chased away from under the bed?

Enough already. Me, not him. I wanted to raise a confident, independent, compassionate, and capable young man. Looks like we're well on our way. It's time I learned to celebrate his bigness.

There will never be such a thing as enough of him.

No matter where he is, where he goes in life, **enough is never**

enough when we love.

Hey, Fifteen
Renee Robbins

"I don't have any wisdom on raising teenagers. It's like dodgeball, except no one wants you on their team, you have to play anyway, and you aren't allowed to throw anything back. And everyone is yelling at you, even the dodgeballs. And you have to wash everyone's uniforms after the game or the world will end. Ask me when it's over." ~This is My Day Job

Sometimes I watch my son sleep, just for a minute before I head to my room for the night, where I hope to escape the anxious dreams that hold me just far enough below the surface to feel suffocated, to break through sweating and breathless, only to slip back under, but never deep enough to get any real rest.

This is fifty-one. Menopause and mortality are conspiring against me. I already know who wins.

He sleeps under two fleece blankets, each made for a much smaller boy – one who is not six foot two with size fourteen feet. I remember he had those blankets with him in the hospital when he had spinal fusion surgery two years ago. I brought them to him when he awoke, still high from the anesthesia, and in so much pain, it hurt to look at him. *I'm so glad I woke up, mom, I was so scared I wouldn't, thank you for being here. I love you, mom. I love you. I love...* and he was out again. And I cried because I never knew how afraid he was. He never said a word.

When you stand beside him, it is sometimes hard to remember that he is still a boy. But he is, for just a while longer. I hear him on his phone, or with his friends, and his awkward, beautiful laugh, sudden and shrill, recalls the boy that was there before, the one who shrieked with joy when tickled and begged *again mama, again, again.* The one I never see anymore. That is not who he is when he is with me. He is distant and curt and sullen. Being a mother to a teenager is a dark place for someone sensitive to exclusion. With the right word he can turn back the clock and make me want to slam the door in his face and refuse to speak to him for the rest of the day, for days, instead of standing there, stung, as I quietly stop helping the person who just angrily told me that he doesn't need me or my help. Again. Who will ask for my help fifteen minutes later, as if it had never happened.

This is fifteen. Adolescence and time are at war in him. We both already know who wins.

He has started making some notably bad decisions. Simultaneously. Consecutively. Sub-sequentially. It's like when he was little, and he used to line up all his rubber ducks on the side of the bathtub, and when he got tired of shooting them off one by one (Pew! Pew! Pew!), he'd swing at them like a baby Godzilla, sweeping them all to the floor in a heap before raising his chubby little arms to the sky with a triumphant "YAAAAAAAAAH!" All ducks, no rows.

This was inevitable, I know. Teenagers will eventually rebel. They will find a way to assert their independence – if you are lucky, it will be with terrible music, and clothing choices that make you cringe. Friends you aren't sure about. But sometimes they show you just how much you don't know, and it will chill you to the bone.

It turns out, this stage of parenting is not at all like the sitcoms of my formative years had indicated. No laugh track, no picture-perfect and wise mom and dad dole out sage advice and consequences in a smug, pithy little package. No cool uncle or wisecracking housekeeper to tsk and roll their eyes, and help turn things around by the time the credits roll, honor-student status intact.

There is no rule book for those moments. No directions for those times where you can see what he can't: that the path of his life, of our lives, can be forever altered in a split second by a choice that he thought was NBD. In one fell swoop, two bewildered parents, an angry teenager and the almost-was whistle of fate.

These won't be the last bad decisions he makes, and if we are being honest, I'm still way ahead in the barely-survived-my-own-teenage-choices department – a revelation that holds very little comfort. In six months, he will be driving a car without me in it, and that is when the terror begins.

Some days I am so ready for this part to be over. To be on the other side of this. I'm ready to be wiser me, prepared to write myself a poignant letter telling me all the things I know now that I wish I had known then. Ready to meet the version of him that most of the time, I know he will become. I am already proud of who he is and who he will be.

But here, in the trenches, there is no respite. You don't know that you have done enough, taught them enough, lived by example enough to save them from themselves at a time when they don't know that is what they need saving from. Tomorrow he could face something you did everything you could to prepare him for, and he could choose wrongly just because he can. You can do everything right, and lose it all anyway.

I sometimes long for the sassy, energetic, and frustrating little boy that had to do what I said. The one I could choose breakfast for, dance in the kitchen with, who gave unexpected hugs and still told me he loved me.

And then I remember that there were times I wished that away, too. He is struggling to break free, and I am learning to let go. I am still a safe space for him, but only when he wants it. For many of the decisions he makes now, my involvement is limited to helping him through the consequences. These are the last days – a time when he is figuring out if, and how much, he wants me in his life. I have to give him the space to fall and pray I still have the reach to catch him if he needs it. And the faith to believe he won't.

We are both hurtling toward the same not-so-distant moment in time – the time when I am no longer there. Figuratively at first, and then literally. Mortality and time are conspiring against us, and we both know who wins in the end.

Hopefully, it's love. Please, let it be love.

For now, I am going to try to remember that he doesn't really want to hurt me. That it's called "growing pains" for a reason. I am going to stand here in the doorway and watch him sleep for a minute more, and remember that no matter what he says, no matter how he acts, he is much more afraid of what comes next than he pretends to be.

And I am going to be here for him when he wakes up.

Parenting While Chronically Ill: Maybe You Did Enough
Cheryl Gottlieb Boxer

"When our children are older, keeping them near is like holding a butterfly in your hands. It's amazing to view their beauty up close. But the real magic is watching their breathtaking flight when you set them free." ~No Sick Days for Mom

A couple of weeks ago, my seventeen-year-old daughter approached me in the kitchen and asked if I'd like to read the assignment she had just completed for her high school creative writing class.

Now when your teenage daughter offers you this kind of access to her life, this glimpse into her creative soul, you don't want to make any sudden moves that might scare her off. In an abundance of caution, I chose not to utter a word. I simply nodded my head and cautiously extended my hand to take the papers she voluntarily offered.

And I read those three pages (typed, double-spaced) slowly and carefully while my daughter waited patiently, her eyes never leaving my face. I could hardly breathe as I finished her paper, and told her honestly it was one of the most beautiful and heartbreaking things I had ever read. I know she saw the tears in my eyes and felt the earnest sincerity of my praise. Buoyed by my accolades and my assurance that her teacher would love the piece, my daughter collected her words and left me alone in that kitchen.

Left me alone and wrecked.

My daughter had written about caring for me during a particularly bad flare-up of my ulcerative colitis. She recounted throwing away platefuls of my uneaten food, hearing me get sick to my stomach behind the closed bathroom door, and helping me walk from the bathroom to my bed when I was too weak to make that short trip unassisted.

To be honest, I have no memory of the particular episode she wrote about.

Perhaps that's because there were so many such episodes over the years — days when I was too sick to make it off our worn denim-blue sofa. When I curled myself into a fetal position to mitigate the pain; my bloated, weak and exhausted body beached on that blue sofa like a whale stranded on the shore.

Over the years I'd read the results of research citing that children of chronically ill parents are often overwhelmed by the responsibility of caring for an ill person, feel restricted in their daily activities, isolate themselves from peer groups, or develop their own health problems.
So I assembled a support system for my kids and hoped I could give them a "normal" childhood. I have a husband who did what he could in the few evening hours he had at home after a long day spent in the office. A devoted mom who helped care for her grandchildren and remained a steady, loving, and supportive presence in their lives as they grew older. Friends who, when I was at my worst, ran errands, carpooled and picked up groceries to stock our refrigerator.

And I hoped and prayed I had done enough. However, my teenage daughter's words left me wondering if I had only created the illusion of a normal childhood. Smoke and mirrors, sleight of hand like the kind my son had mastered so many years ago when as a little boy he performed elaborate magic shows at our kitchen table. But illusions and tall tales have a short shelf life. I wondered how long the jig had been up.

I look at my children today, and I see young adults who are thriving. My daughter, a junior in high school, is a trumpet-blowing, free-thinking, reptile-loving, outspoken feminist. My son, 350 miles away on a college campus, is spreading his wings, meeting new people, traveling to far-away places, and keeping his mom on her toes and her heart in her throat. And I would venture to say experiencing life with a chronically ill parent has endowed these young adults with certain extraordinary gifts.

They learned that vulnerability is not a weakness. On my worst days, I could not have gotten by without help from the people in my life who loved and cared about me. My children observed this early on, and as young adults, they still appreciate when someone is there for them with a kind word or a helping hand. They realize that it truly does take a village, and they actively seek out these connections in their lives. My teenagers don't shy away from needing others or from being needed.

My kids are excellent bullshit detectors. No amount of makeup or false giddiness can throw these young adults off the trail. They know exactly how to see through a shiny veneer and uncover the truth that lies beneath. They are incredibly attuned to the feelings of others, and instinctively know if someone is hurting or afraid.

And my teenagers know that some days will be simply, terribly, awful. There is no getting around the fact that life is messy. My young adults have seen some very bad, dark days. But they also know that the following day, or maybe the following week, things can be better. They are resilient, optimistic, and strong. I feel confident they will truly relish the good days that come their way and will have the conviction to tackle the difficult and messy ones as well.

On any given day parenting is hard. It is frightening. Parenting while chronically ill is particularly brutal. Knowing that our illness has changed who our children are is the most heartbreaking realization for a sick parent.

And yet, it has been my greatest blessing to watch these children, with their unordinary childhood, grow into teens who are doing extraordinary things. Where I saw myself lacking my children simply saw me loving them. And while it pains me still that I could not give them everything, I'm pretty sure if you ask them, they'll tell you it was more than enough.

Goody-Two-Shoes Barbie
DC Stanfa

"My mother always said that payback was going to be a bitch when I became a mom—since I was such a troublemaking teen. My daughter was an A student and a band geek. I'm praying that my troublemaking gene doesn't skip a generation." ~DC Stanfa, Author

I had officially logged more time at my daughter's high school than I did at my own alma mater, and it was only Cori's junior year. It was not due to being summoned to her principal's office to discuss behavior problems like my mother was so often for me. In fact, I almost didn't graduate, due to truancy. I didn't skip all classes equally, but often enough. I regularly walked out of social studies after intense arguments with my card-carrying Communist teacher—not knowing that he marked me absent each time I left.

On the contrary, my daughter, Cori, never skipped school. She loved school. She hated to miss a class, even if she wasn't feeling well. She was also obsessive about never being a minute tardy. The reason I had better attendance at Cori's school is that I was there repeatedly to applaud her. Whether it was to witness her induction into the National Honors Society, or to attend numerous chorus concerts, or to attend football games to watch her color guard/ band performances—and all the banquets for each—congratulatory hand-clapping (instead of the hand-wringing I caused my mother) always concluded the event.

If witnesses had not been present as she emerged from my vagina, family and friends would not believe she is my daughter.

Ironic that the skipping-school gene skipped a generation—as did the hitchhiking-to-bars-by-the-time-you-are-sixteen chromosome, and the stealing-your-parent's-car-and-driving-it-around the block trait (hitting three parked cars and a truck along the way) at the age of thirteen.

Thank you, God!

My mother told me that having a teenage daughter would certainly be the payback bitch I deserved because of the bad karma I created during my misspent youth. I guess that payback will be in another lifetime, in which I have six juvenile delinquents; hell-hath-no-fury-like-this woman's spawn. Yikes. I may have to denounce my belief in reincarnation.

In this life, motherhood has been Heaven-on-Earth, especially compared to the real hell I put my parents through. When I mentally compared, and contrasted my high school experience to Cori's, I decided it had to be written down so that when her own teenager doesn't measure up to the standard of excellence she created, Cori can find some comfort in placing the blame where it belongs, squarely on the chip on my shoulder—which in high school was more like a two-by-four.

Occasionally, I take one of those stupid Facebook quizzes like Which Gilligan's Island character are you? (The Skipper, but I think they meant The Stripper.) And Who Were You in High School? Cori took that one too. She was Most Likely to Succeed while I was Most Likely to Smoke Weed. Cori's quiz, Which Barbie are You? was the inspiration for the title of this chapter. By the way, I am Black Sheep of the Barbie Family.

The amazing contrast of Cori—the classic overachiever to my high school underachievement—has allowed me to experience vicariously what it is like to have the opposite experience growing up. It's like my daughter did a do-over of my teen years for me, rewriting tragedy into her/our triumph.

For me, high school was hapless: frizzy hair and a face full of acne covered with industrial amounts of Clearasil (which did not provide the aphrodisiac effect I'd hoped for) in my search of male companionship. I was dateless and bitter, jealous of both my sisters who had real, not imaginary, boyfriends. I also hated every girl who was blessed with boobs and the boyfriends who just might be touching that boobage.

For Cori, high school was straight as, a slew of great friends and an assortment of extracurricular activities—none of which were illegal. Mountain Dew was the drug of choice for Cori and her crew. She could have written a book titled Good Clean Fun, which, to my generation, sounds like an oxymoron.

The truth is, I should read that book someday.
When Cori was about sixteen, we were at her pediatrician's office.

"So, Denise, have you had the 'don't drink and don't smoke talk'?" the doctor asked.

"Yes, but she still can't get me to quit," I replied.

When Cori was a senior, I allowed her to glance at my senior yearbook. I figured that since she was well into her own senior year, she likely wouldn't fall under the influence of all the "partying" references my classmates had penned. No, she didn't throw down her color guard flag in favor of a bong. Nor was she surprised at all the mentions of drinking and toking scribbled along with signatures. Cori was, however, shocked by one thing.

"Mom, you were the president of DECA?" (Distributive Education Clubs of America was an association for marketing, hospitality, fashion, and other business areas.)
"Yeah, so what?" I answered, noting an obvious tone of disbelief

in her voice

"Well, I'm just surprised you were president of anything because you didn't seem to care enough about anything in high school."

Was she calling me apathetic?

I did care about some things. In fact, I cared very passionately about avoiding class as much as possible. The DECA. Class of which I was president consisted of girls, most of them friends who wanted to be in the same class, so we could all regularly and collectively skip it. Thus, DECA became Don't Even Consider Attending. We often met at Frisch's Big Boy for breakfast and would show up to class at our leisure, claiming we'd just had a board meeting. Our advisor was an ex-retail buyer in her rookie year of teaching — poor woman. I'm pretty sure we're the reason it was also her last.

As part of some of Cori's college applications, parents were expected to write a "brag sheet." I first listed some of her experiences and achievements as an outline of the essay. Then, for comic relief, I listed my high school achievements next to hers. No, I did not include mine in her essay.

Cori: Captain of the Color Guard

DC: Did mock modeling poses for baked friends

Cori: Honors Chorus Concerts

DC: Rod Stewart and Rolling Stones concerts

Cori: Physics Geothermal Project

DC: Crafted a ceramic bong in art class

Cori: Treasurer of the National Honor Society

DC: Rolled joints for friends for extra money

Cori: President of the Spanish Honor Society

DC: See DECA above

Cori: Green Club

DC: Club Cannabis

Cori: AP Euro study parties

DC: Learned how to shoot a beer at a party

Cori: Volunteer at the Literacy Council

DC: Made baked beans for senior skip-day picnic
However, Cori and I had one commonality of both of our high school experiences. We talked about it several times.

"You know, it's like that drawing of two circles—in this case, they'd only overlap slightly at one tiny, tiny point," I once commented.

"It's called a Venn diagram, Mom," Cori explained.

Anyway, that point where we intersect was "dateless." While she had neither frizzy hair nor acne nor any other reason not to have a boyfriend, like I did, she still didn't have one. Regardless of dates, she and her friends went en-masse to homecoming dances and proms, proving girls know how to have fun. Ultimately, Cori loved the school experience so much that she made a career of it. Cori became a Spanish teacher. And we both hope and pray she never has a student, nor a son or daughter, like me.

I'm His Mom and Not His Sister

Elyse Orecchio

"I still feel like I'm playing the role of parent. Will I ever consider myself an actual adult instead of the drama kid improvising a really, really long scene?" ~Elyse Orecchio, Writer

The first diaper I ever changed was my son's. I learned how to be Theo's mom while learning Calculus and Astronomy at school.

What do you think when you hear nineteen-year-old mom? Depending on where you live, maybe you think it's young but not so teen mom young. But here in New York City, the shock factor is high. For perspective, I'm thirty-five, and many of my high-school friends are starting to think about maybe sort of having children.

Theo and I were a duo even before he was born. I was in an undergrad theatre program, and because I already had Theo's name picked out in utero, he became a character in our acting classes. My friends addressed him in improv scenes: *Don't shoot—watch out for Theo!*

And because I was still in college when Theo was born and time was flexible, we were always on the go. I didn't have a group of mom friends then. I didn't do particularly baby-friendly activities (how would I have known what they were? This was before Mommy Poppins was a thing). I did everything I'd always done, but while wearing Theo. He was really just an extension of me. When I think about our time together in those days, I think of walking the city for hours and how he always fell asleep on the seven train between the Grand Central and Vernon Jackson stops.

Fifteen years passed, and while I'm no longer a teenager, people sure love to tell me I look like one. When I go to my son's high school, I brace myself to be mistaken for a student. I know, I know. No one likes that annoying douchebag who complains about looking too young. Oh, poor baby! We should all have that problem!

But look. Often I mention I'm a mom, and the reaction is, "Wait, you have kids?"

Not little kids, mind you, but kids. Period.

I drop the next doozy: My oldest is fifteen.

Next come the squeal, the dropped jaw, the demand for pictures (proof). The proclamation to anyone within earshot: "SHE HAS KIDS." And then the interrogation.

How old were you? Nineteen.

Was he planned? No.

Did you consider abortion? Yes.
Is the dad still in the picture? My husband, yes (though clearly that's the wrong answer and the question was constructed to make me feel less-than).

My little boy is six-foot-one with a mustache and proper teen-aged wispy sideburns. He has my long neck, bushy eyebrows, and goofy smile. On Saturday mornings, we play Mario Party while my husband and daughter sleep in. Theo wakes up early like I do. Theo is a rule follower like I am. We are both hopelessly punctual. He shares my good manners and affection for felines. He looks like me; he is part of me.

I feel self-conscious when he and I walk down the street. I can feel the instant-analysis as they wonder just what are we to each other. I don't post many photos of the two of us on social media as protection against the usual refrain:

"You don't look like his mom. You could be his sister!"

People mean well, they say. It's a compliment, they say. But here's the thing.

I am his mom and not his sister because I cried over the first stretch mark on my belly. I was far into the pregnancy and diligent with cocoa butter, and I'd thought I was one of the lucky ones—that maybe I had a chance to go into my twenties with an unmarked stomach. Then there I was in our studio apartment in Queens watching *Spirited Away* and noticed the lone slash of bluish red. Many more would follow. Over the years, I came to regard the marks as the road map to motherhood they are. But damn straight I cried over that first one.

I am his mom and not his sister because my left boob is smaller than my right—did the little jerk suck unevenly?!

I am his mom and not his sister because when he was two, he was so constipated and red-faced that I gloved up and pulled the hardened cluster of shit out of his little butt. I felt the relief as though it were my own.

I am his mom and not his sister because when he was three, he couldn't fall asleep without playing with my belly button.

I am his mom and not his sister because I made him an actual sister. When we put baby Melody in his four-year-old arms, it was out with me and in with her. From that moment on, she would be his best friend. His number-one. And because I am his mother, nothing could please me more.

I am his mom and not his sister because I attend IEP meetings each year. I got him his first evaluation before he even turned two. I was barely old enough to drink legally, and I was working with therapists who couldn't promise my baby would ever talk. He was diagnosed with Pervasive Development Disorder (PDD), and two years later, we got the official autism verdict.

I am his mom and not his sister because I commemorated his first word with a Christmas ornament that says, "Bapple."
I am his mom and not his sister because I'm his first phone call when the subway is screwed up, and he needs help finding an alternate route to school, to his youth theater group, to go get a haircut.

Common conceptions about young moms include missing out on partying or losing your shot at your dreams, but for me, really the worst part of the gig is that the New York State Regents exams aren't a distant enough memory and it's bringing me serious PSTD (post-standardized-testing disorder) getting Theo the review books.

Of course, there are advantages to my childhood not being too far behind me. For example, I have an affinity to video games my older mom counterparts don't generally share. While many of them roll their eyes at gaming husbands, I fully expect the next generation of moms to be hitting the consoles with their kids; I just got a head start.

If I sound too much like a cool mom, don't worry. I can't keep up with the newer games like Minecraft or the weird YouTube channels the crazy kids are watching—what is Fortnite anyway?—so I'm approaching cane-shaking status in spite of myself. I'm still down for a game of Mario Party anytime, though. The little Italian plumber's staying power has been fierce.

Watch out—here comes the unqualified psych-evaluation portion of this piece.

What if the real reason I'm so sensitive to comments that I can't possibly be a mom is that deep down I share the same fear?

Who am I to sign a permission slip, or give an allowance, or declare a curfew? Yeah, I have a career, a home, and a family, but after fifteen years I still feel like I'm playing the role of parent. Will I ever consider myself an actual adult instead of the drama kid improvising a really, really long scene?

But hey, "adulting" wasn't even a word when I had Theo. We're all making up shit as we go, as Theo will do when he's a parent. By the way, he's already picked out names for his future kids—Emily and Jeremy—so if he finds any takers, look out for my essay, "I'm his grandma and not his mom."

I Forgot To Raise Him to Be a Man

Anne Metz

"I'm new to this parenting a teen thing, and honestly, I have no idea what I'm doing. But my son is new to this being a teen thing too. So we'll do what we've always done, figure it out as we go along, together." ~Once Upon a Mom

I forgot to raise my son to be a man. And now he's thirteen. There are only five years left until he is officially an adult. I have so little time and much to my dismay, so little influence left.

These last five years. These are the years when he will be rolling his eyes at me. Assuming he knows better. He will be looking to his friends for guidance, validation, and acceptance. I fear I've lost my impact over him, just as I am realizing that I have so much left to teach him about what it is to be a good man.

I want him to be a good, decent man like his father. I want to guide him to embrace all the qualities that I admire in his dad. I want him to be honest, hardworking, loving, sacrificial, kind, strong, and respectful. But I forgot. I forgot to raise my son to be a man. To teach him the things that are important about life like independence, responsibility, accountability, respect, and hard work.

I spent so much time teaching him smaller lessons, things little kids need to know. And now I'm caught wondering if it was enough. I am questioning myself. Wishing I had taught him the big lessons.

But instead, I fear I may have wasted my time with small things.

I taught him how to be independent, how to dress himself and brush his teeth, and as he got older, how to straighten his room and do his laundry.

I taught him to play nicely with others. To be kind and not to lash out in anger. I showed him how to give everyone a second chance. To let friends know when they hurt his feelings and to apologize when he hurt theirs. As he got older, I taught him to stand up to bullies and stick up for other children. Not to judge other people by their looks or their social status and not to care what other people thought of him.

I taught him to be honest. Not to tell lies of admission or spread gossip. To be truthful when he makes mistakes and to try to repair them.

I taught him to be safe. To look both ways before crossing the street and to wear a helmet when riding his bike. I had him memorize our phone numbers and gave him a list of trusted adults.

I taught him responsibility. That if he loses a library book, he must find it or pay the fee. That if he doesn't do his homework, he won't get good grades.

I taught him good manners. To wait until all people are served before eating. To hold the door for others. I showed him how Daddy walks on the street side of the sidewalk when he is with his family.

I taught him how to be healthy. To eat fruit and veggies and to find an activity that he likes for exercise.

I taught him about God. To say his prayers and thank God for his blessings.

My son used to look up at me with his chubby dimpled cheeks and his big brown eyes, open to all my lessons and advice as if they were coming from the source itself. He used to absorb it all and take it all as fact. And now he's a teen. His cheeks are no longer chubby, though the dimple is still there. His beautiful brown eyes are not as big, and he no longer looks at me with pure admiration and affinity; he is beginning to question my expertise.
There is a barrier growing between us. A barrier of a shut bedroom door, of eyes that are focused on tablets and video games, and of new friends. It feels like a forest growing between us, and my guidance is no longer able to navigate him through the trees. Time is moving at a lightning pace, my son feels so far away, and all the while new vines and trees shoot up in the jungle between us. There's little time and little space for new lessons.

And so I hope it was enough...my simple lessons.

Was teaching him to be a good friend in grade school enough to help him continue to maintain healthy relationships in high school and beyond?

Was teaching him to look both ways before he crosses the street enough to remind him to be safe in new and possibly dangerous situations?

Was teaching him to say his prayers at night enough to encourage him to have a relationship with God that will sustain him through hardships?

Will it be enough? I hope so. Because there isn't much time left, and honestly, could I have done it differently? Would I have told my sweet five-year-old boy about safety issues beyond his maturity level? Probably not. So I hope and pray that it's enough.

I hope it's enough and though I can't be sure, I tend to think that it just might be. Because when you think about it, these small lessons are the big lessons. I taught my son that these things are important: safety, honesty, good friendships, responsibility, and a strong relationship with God. As he gets older, he'll have more opportunity to experience these lessons in new environments and adult situations. But he knows these are the important things...because I taught him.

Kids are meant to grow away from us so that jungle, it's not necessarily a bad thing; it's the distance my son needs from me as he figures out how to be a man on his own. He has these small lessons with him, and I pray that he remembers them all. But it won't stop me from trying to guide him and teach him how to be a man. I'll wait for the quiet moments, for a clearing in the trees. I'll send him more lessons, and I'll hope it's enough.

His First Middle School Dance

Lynne Getz

"Parenting my teenage son is exhausting and amazing and frustrating and beautiful. It's the ultimate paradox." ~ Like a Mother

Last Friday night, my thirteen-year-old seventh-grader attended his first middle school dance. He wore khaki pants with a pink button-down Oxford shirt that his grandmother picked out, because, as she said, "real men wear pink." He also begrudgingly wore the blue and white plaid tie she picked for him, completing the outfit that made him look like he stepped out of the pages of a Ralph Lauren catalog. But underneath the preppy clothes, he was also wearing a diaper.

My son is not your typical seventh-grader. He was born with a rare chromosomal deletion. A small piece of genetic material is missing from the tip of the small arm of his sixth chromosome. The syndrome doesn't have a fancy name, just a series of numbers and letters that make most people's eyes glaze over. Those missing genes have led to many challenges for my son. His is hearing and vision-impaired, non-verbal, intellectually disabled, unable to chew his food, incapable of being toilet-trained, and very small for his age—only a couple inches taller than his six-year-old brother.

This was also not your typical middle school dance. This was the Buddy Ball, a dance hosted by the middle school chapter of Best Buddies International, an organization dedicated to building friendships between those with and without intellectual and developmental disabilities (IDDs), as well as promoting integrative employment, leadership development, and inclusive living for those with IDDs.

The day of the dance, I was a mess—stressed and anxious. Perhaps that is how all moms feel before a child's first dance, but I don't know that yet. My other two children are younger, so my first experiences with milestones as my children age are always atypical. But my guess is that my stress and anxiety were a little different. Students from nine middle schools attended the dance: both children with IDDs and Buddies, neurotypical students who choose to join the Best Buddies clubs at their schools. The teachers and staff who hosted did an incredible job! It reminded me of attending my own middle school dances thirty years ago, and I was so happy to see all the kids having an amazing time. Unlike my childhood experiences though, there were options for kids who couldn't handle the sensory overload of the dance floor, such as carnival games, a craft room, and a movie playing in a quiet room. My son didn't really want to dance, but we did get him to join a conga line before the night ended. Most of the time, we wandered from room to room, checking to see who was there and what was happening.

As my son entered each new room, the kids who knew him immediately approached him. They came over, said hello, and offered a high-five with a smile. Their greetings were simple, but genuine and heartfelt. They were inclusive and welcoming to the students they knew, and to those from the other schools as well. They all seemed genuinely happy to be there. They were dancing and having fun, just like middle-schoolers should at a dance.

As I watched the Buddies at the dance, I was both grateful and jealous. It's a strange feeling to both admire and resent a group of middle-schoolers. I was simultaneously incredibly grateful they were participating in an important program that helps them learn empathy and the value of inclusion, but I couldn't help but look at them and imagine all the things my son should be doing at the same age.

Tiffany O'Connor

The reality of his differences sneaks up and bites me sometimes, and I can't help but wince at the pain. But I hid my tears, and I kept my focus on the kindness of those amazing kids.

Parenting a child with special needs is emotionally and physically exhausting. Even though he is chronologically a teenager, he's still very much like a toddler. And I worry about him, constantly, in his toddler-like state, venturing into the world. A world that seems to be getting less and less kind to those who are different or unusual or strange. I worry about how the world will treat all of my children, and I'm sure you worry about how it will treat yours too. This is where you can help us both.

You can teach your teenager about my teenager. I'm sure that when they were little, you taught them to be kind to others. You probably taught them about differences, and you likely told them not to stare. You told them that God, or whomever, made my son that way, and left it at that. It sounds nice, and that was what you knew how to do at the time. But now, I need you to do more.

I need you to teach your teenager to include others. That part about not staring? Forget that. Well, it's still not good to stare, but they need to look at their atypical peers and engage with them. This is not about what they shouldn't do, but about what they can do. They can say hello and have a conversation. If the other person is non-verbal or has another way of communicating, they can ask teachers or helpers how to communicate. They can learn how to talk to them. And they can learn about them—what they like, what they don't like. If your teen doesn't understand something, they can ask. Really, it's okay to ask, as long as it's done with curiosity and not judgment. It's far better than making assumptions. They can become part of programs like Best Buddies, a program which is expanding and growing in schools across the United States and internationally. If their school doesn't have a program, they can ask about starting one, or they can ask if there's a less formal way they can participate in inclusive programming. Maybe it's through a sport or an after-school program. Maybe it's at your place of worship. There are so many opportunities to make a difference. Teach your child to find them!

I would never have asked for this life. Being the parent of a teenager with special needs is really hard, and I have days when I ask, "Why me?" But there are moments when I see the pure light in my son, and I know that others see it too. I remind myself of all the good that has come into my life because of him, and I know he brings good into the lives of others, like the kids in Best Buddies. I know I am better because of him, and I know they will be better as well.

Your child will be better too.

Moving Toward Adulthood
Judy Daniell

"I highly recommend getting a dog during your children's teen years. It's not to teach them responsibility, but it's so someone is happy to see you when you get home." ~ Judy Daniell, Writer

We're in the middle of a season at our home. Lest you be distracted by the cleats and mud and baseball bats and footballs and hoop-shooting and teenage boy stink, that's not the type of season I'm talking about. We're raising a house full of boys amid a season full of change and newness and goodbyes and uncertainty and excitement.

Isn't this the stuff that is life? A culmination of all the feelings, at the same time. Life is lovely and tragic, messy and beautiful, exciting and devastating…and that all could be on some random Saturday. Meanwhile, my husband and I expected to raise respectable and honorable men while we're still trying to wrap our heads around the complicated beauty of life.

For a long time, I did not enjoy the overlapping emotions that life gave me. I wanted things to be cut and dry. Simplicity over complicated. Quick over long and drawn out. When it's time to be happy, I want to be all-around happy. A time for uncertainty is short and met with a quick resolution so that I can get back to my comfort zone, and I can easily say, "Wow. Glad that's over and look at all I learned from it." {Hastily dusts my hands off and moves on to the next thing.}

Quite frankly, for a long time, I kept waiting to hit the cruise control on my life…when all my hard work paid off, and I could just kick back and enjoy the downhill coast for the rest of the trip. But that's not how this works. There's no cruise control on life. So instead of acting put out when life does what life does (because it will), I'm choosing to be open to what life has in store and learning to embrace the complexity of emotions that comes along with the ride. And somehow, I'm working on passing these lessons onto kids who spend their days jamming out to music, heading to practice and playing video games and make fleeting appearances when hunger pangs strike. Their lives are filled up with school and sports and friends. But underneath it all, is this season that we're in. And it's seasons like these that will grow these boys up into men. It's part of their metamorphosis, the part that looks painful and hard but is absolutely necessary. Similar to any good biologist, my job is to not rush the process, or try to intervene during this phase that will surely bring about growth, even though my heart is breaking at times.

"How are the boys taking the news? Are you worried about moving during high school?"

We moved last summer. We pulled up stakes and took our kids away from the home we lived in for nearly eight years and the place they called home.

So, hell yes, I'm worried. I'm a parent. That's what I do.

I worry if I'm doing it right.

I worry they won't be ready when the time comes.

I worry about sending them out into a world where they will certainly face difficulty and strife, and I worry that maybe their lives were too safe and precious in our home and they won't be ready when the time comes.

Since part of my job requirement is to prepare them for this cruel, tragic, beautiful world, using moments of pain and discomfort to move the needle on their maturity is one of the hardest parts of parenting.

My boys live a very comfortable and safe life. If the most difficult thing they have to do is uproot their lives, move to another town forty-five minutes away from their friends and teammates with their parents who adore each other, into a home filled with love and encouragement…then so be it.

Because, if we're honest, that's the easiest way to do hard things in this life…surrounded by a safety net of love and support. It's almost as if we have to manufacture hardship for these kids in order to ensure they develop resilience for later in life. If moving with their parents and brothers is the most difficult thing my kids will endure, they'll be better for it.

And they are all learning to navigate the newness of it all. They're learning to navigate an entirely new social scene, athletic fields, and teaching philosophies. Some transitions have gone smoother than others, and there may have been tears (mostly mine), but I know that with every bump in the road and hurdle overcome, these boys are learning who they are and learning to believe in themselves.

"What an opportunity. What an opportunity for your growth."

A year ago, before we even knew a move was on the horizon, my husband and I were having a late-night heart-to-heart with one of the boys. It began with him recounting an event that led to him recounting a series of similar events that led to the realization that he was in the midst of a moment that would surely begin to define the man he becomes.

And as much as we wanted to gloss over it, do the hard work for him, and otherwise make it go away, that would only damage and prolong his growth process.
Instead, my husband told him, "What an opportunity. What an opportunity for your growth." We wanted him to know that we fully loved and supported him, but that he would need to the

hard work.

And he did.

And it was beautiful.

And now we're doing it again. With all three of them this time. They continue to push through the discomfort of change, push through their own boundaries of how to cope with difficult life situations and are learning what they are capable of accomplishing, moving that needle of maturity toward adulthood. And my husband and I are right here, cheering them on because we believe in them enough to watch them struggle through the process, figure it out, and grow.

The Basic Dad
Shannon Carpenter

"If you are not sure if you are being insulted by your teenager, just watch how quickly they whisper to their friends." ~ Hossman at Home

"Dad, you're so basic," my thirteen-year-old daughter says from the backseat of the minivan. Her two friends laugh beside her.

Honestly, I'm not sure how to respond because I don't really know if that is an insult. It sounds like one mostly because of the way she said it. There is an assholery tone to her voice. I mean, I can pretty much hear the eyeball roll at the end of the sentence. Originally, this was going to be a nice drive to drop them off at a skating party. Now it's a journey about teen vocabulary.

"What is basic?" I caveman grunt at my daughter and her alpha tribe. Since her last birthday, I understand less and less of what she says. It's as if she is speaking a new language that's filled with emoji's and acronyms sent across text messages that remind me of cave drawings in the south of France. There are only two words that I understand anymore. "Whatever" and "embarrassing." Mainly because those are used more than any other.

"Nothing," she giggles in the back.

"Seriously, I want to know what it means."

"Whatever."

See! That word, I understand. It means "I'm done talking with you, Dad."

"Is it an insult? It sounds like an insult?" I ask.

"It's not, really," says one of the followers.

"It's not good, though," says another one.

"It's you're music, Dad. It's basic."

My knuckles go white as they grip the steering wheel. Even Flow by Pearl Jam blares through the speakers like heaven's trumpets, and I turn it up. I'll admit, I'm hurt. This is the thing about teenagers. They speak before thinking. I believe the technical term is "blurting out of the pie-hole, insensitive remarks before thinking." I'm sure I read that in a scientific paper somewhere. My daughter is too young to understand that you never, ever, insult a man's music. Grunge is unassailable.

"Turn it down!" they all say.

I turn it up instead. I'm not proud of it. It was more of an emotional reaction than of a well thought out fatherly one. What I should have done is stopped the car and given an excellent lecture about the musical influences of bands like Pearl Jam and Nirvana. I could use diagrams and charts to explain why Grunge is the best music ever. We could learn the art of the air guitar. We used to do that a lot, and honestly, I miss those days. I miss that girl.

"Please!" my daughter says.

I wait a beat and then give them relief. They laugh in the back.

"Ok, seriously, how can I not be basic? Give it to me," I say. It's like I kicked a hornet's nest in the backseat. The responses come rapid fire.

"Wear cooler clothes!"

"Better music!"

"A nicer car!"

"Grow hair!"

OUCH!

"Dad," my daughter begins her lecture, and I'm assuming she will use diagrams, "it's just that you are like every other dad out there. Ya know, basic."

"Honey, I'm an at-home-dad," I say, "There aren't many out there like me. I gave up everything to be with you." I like laying down the guilt from time to time. Somedays I do it just out of habit.

"Not that. I mean, you drive a minivan, and on the weekends you do yard work."

"Well, the yard isn't going to fix HOA complaints on its own!" I laugh at my little joke. They don't.

"Dad! It's just a stupid yard," my daughter says.

Woah, Woah, woah. First my music now my yard? For a minute, I consider slamming on the breaks and making them go home and mow. The other two kids aren't even mine, but it sounds like they need some good life lessons. My father's instinct flares up, and I swear I almost do it. But then I remember that I need to be patient. This is a long journey, and it's only just begun.

I figure I've got another four to five years of this. Of passive-aggressive statements and insulting tones. And I don't want to run my daughter off, to widen the now canyon between us. Win hearts and minds and then make them mow the yard. That's the ticket. In my mind, I schedule some outdoor work for this Saturday.

"So, my hair, which I have no control over, and my yard, and my music. You three want to keep going or do you want to cut your losses now?" Nirvana's Smells Like Teen Spirit comes on the radio.

"You dress like all the other dads, too," my daughter says. "Like, your sweater."

I audibly gasp. You can hear me suck in all the air available in the car. My grandmother would say that I have the vapors, and I should probably lay down for a bit. Now I really am angry.

"What the hell is wrong with my sweater?" I say.

"It's just a blue sweater. Every dad wears a sweater," one of them responds, the bravest of the three.

My big blue dad sweater, earned through countless sleepless nights over the last thirteen years. It's my varsity letter jacket, a symbol that yes, now I am Father. Be in awe. Wounded, I do the only thing that I can.

I pipe a guitar solo from Sound Garden to the backseat, and I drink in their protests.

"No more! The music is so basic! Where is Ariana Grande?"

"I don't know who that is!" I reply.

"Of course you don't because you are basic!"

I hear the shutter of phone cameras going off and know my basicness is headed to Instagram. But you can't rip apart the greatest rock ever created. Nirvana, Pearl Jam, and the short-lived Temple Of The Dog. They are not classics, nay, they are still as relevant today as they were twenty-four years ago. Back when I had hair, and I trained in yard mowing. And to trash the very sweater that I have earned through hardship? That's too far. Way too far.

I pull up to the roller skating rink. Flop sweat pours off my brow, and my emotional wounds run deep. The girls pile out as a pack of vipers ready to strike at the next fun-loving dad and his sweater. I roll down all the windows as they try to blend into the crowd of other teenagers. I try to be above stuff like this, to let the hurt go. She is my daughter, and I love her so much. It physically hurts sometimes in my heart when she is not near me. I owe her my best.

But you should never insult a dad's sweater.

I drive away slow as a turtle to the hard beats of Vaseline by Stone Temple Pilots just as they get to a pack of boys. I see the girls wince as heads pivot my way.

I'm basically being embarrassing… and they deserve it.
But as the guitar riff starts and echoes off the surrounding buildings, I see my daughter briefly break into an air guitar. It's quick but it happened when everyone looked at me. When I was the center of attention and no eyes were on her. At that moment, all was right with the world.

There she is. That's my girl.

I'm Ready When You Are
Marybeth Bock

"When raising teens, always be armed with these three things: The phrase "I love you too much to argue." A healthy sense of humor. A hefty supply of wine." ~Marybeth Bock, Writer

I have always been a punctual person. Being late for something stresses me out. This is most likely because I was raised by a father who was a pilot. I grew up with the understanding that when you were supposed to be somewhere, you arrived on time.

Once I became a parent myself, my rigid standards for punctuality abruptly came to a screeching halt. Every parent can remember those early days, when you finally had your baby all bundled up, belted into their car seat, covered with a fluffy, little blanket, and before you could even finish backing out of your driveway, you heard that distinctly, horrifying sound — DIAPER BLOW-OUT. Twenty minutes later you were attempting to depart for the second time, sweaty and annoyed, and now very late.

Then came the toddler and pre-school years, when your patience was tried about every two minutes of your waking hours. You knew you could get your kids out the door so much faster if you did all the things, but you also knew how important it was for them to learn to tie their shoelaces themselves, and put their snack into their backpack and zip it up, and brush their teeth, and, and, and…

In time, the "leaving" routine in our house developed into me hovering somewhere near the door to the garage, usually picking up stray toys and socks, and declaring in a song-song-y voice to my kids, "I'm ready to go whenever you are." They came to understand that this meant, "Please try to hurry and finish up whatever prep you're still doing and get your butt into the car."

I'd be ready and waiting for them to drive to school. Or to baseball practice. Or to a Girl Scout meeting. Or a trip to the craft store to buy poster board for the project that was due tomorrow! It seemed I was always ready first, and the two of them took their own, sweet time.

"Just a minute while I finish this game, Mom."

"Hold on; I have to find my folder."

"I gotta go to the bathroom first!"

"Hey, do you know where my sweatshirt is?"

And seemingly in a flash, the middle school years arrived. And one Friday morning before school, as we were rushing around the kitchen, my daughter casually mentioned that she was going to the movies that night.
WITH A BOY…

And I thought, oh geez, am I ready for this?

The thoughts that began to form and swirl in my brain were inexplicable. What will she do if he tries to awkwardly kiss her and she's not ready? What will happen if he tells other boys she did something with him that she didn't do?

I suddenly felt like I needed to sit her down and discuss dating and young love and all the possible scenarios she might find herself in, in that dark movie theater. I felt this urge to jump online and find several reputable websites, and perhaps create a PowerPoint presentation with statistics and multi-colored pie charts and graphs. The worry center of my brain kicked into overdrive. I most definitely wasn't ready for the murky world of teen dating quite yet.

I casually broached the subject of teen-boy expectations that afternoon and was quickly shut down, "I'll be fine, Mom. I know how to take care of myself." Teen speak for: I'm ready. Chill out. And so, there began a succession of similarly bold behaviors with pacifying proclamations. Freshman year dances where she would then spend the night at a new friend's house afterward. Who was driving them? Would the friend's parents be home? Was there going to be alcohol?

I'M NOT READY!
"It's all good, Mom. We're not stupid."

Next came the sunny day she first walked out the door, fresh driver's license tucked into a ridiculous Duct Tape "wallet," got into the car (with a stick-shift!) and readied herself to drive off alone. Completely alone. Out into the big, wide world. Where are you going? Are you taking the freeway? Do you know what exit to get off at? Do you have the number for the roadside assistance?

I'M NOT READY!

"I'm a safe driver, Mom, please don't worry."

And two years later, came the punch to my gut. The day she decided to attend college on the complete opposite side of the country. Are you sure you want to be that far away? Will you be alright not knowing anyone there? Do you understand it takes two flights to get there?

I'M NOT READY!

"I am so excited to go to school there!"

I could not deny her that experience nor even think to shut down that unabashed joy. The script had been flipped, and I had become the dawdler. The straggler. The lethargic foot-dragger.

Looking back with parental hindsight, I rationally knew she was ready for those milestones, but how had we gotten there so very quickly? Your brain can know something is factual, yet your heart can behave like that of a five-year-old, still laying on the floor in her room, lining up *Littlest Pet Shop* animals and humming a song from *Disney's Tarzan* soundtrack, not quite ready to move on to the next activity. The teen years are unique that way.

Initially, we spend long and tiresome days and nights pushing our kids to advance to the next stage. Exhausted new parents speak longingly about the "sleeping through the night" breakthrough. We coax and encourage those first wobbly steps, recording their progress with proud cheering. We carefully chart with gold star stickers and hand over small prizes for using that tiny, plastic potty. We persuade them to try out for the soccer team or to take dance lessons, or coding classes, reassuring them it will be fun and there will be new friends.

Many of us unexpectedly get wary as soon as our kids become teenagers. Perhaps it is because we can remember our teen years so easily. We can vividly picture where we were and what music may have been playing when we experienced our first awkward kiss. We can remember what outfit we were wearing when someone called us out publicly or caused us some emotional pain. Teen angst can leave subterranean and lasting scars in our psyche. It's why John Hughes movies like *The Breakfast Club* and *Pretty in Pink* appeal to both teens and adults. We can intensely recall how those characters felt: shamed, left out, inadequate, or frightened.

As parents, we may begin to want to shield our teens from the fears, and the awkwardness, and the heartaches. They start to feel bolder and to jump at the chance for more freedom, as we may begin to pull back on the reins. We fear that we need to release now so that they can experience their own - to be fully in the fear and the awkwardness, and to move through it.

Our instinct is to protect them from harms, both physical and emotional. We can somewhat prepare them for both, but the teen years are for exploration and delving into new challenges. We will never be able to prevent all those harms. When they feel ready, we need to allow them to make their own mistakes and to build up a supply of courage. And we need to be mindful that they are statistically safer and better educated about harms than we were as teenagers.

I will never forget the warm evening that my seventeen-year-old daughter was set to drop me off at a friend's house on her way to a fall football game. I was still upstairs getting my shoes on when I heard her sing to me from downstairs, car keys jingling in her hand,

"Mom…. I'm ready when you are."

And she was.

Parenting a Struggling Teen
Lyndee Brown

"If your child speaks in *grunts* they are probably a teenage boy" ~#Lifewithboys

Right now, I am writing this story with a smile on my face because my son and I have made it. We made it through two years of tears, anger, frustration, and the complete and utterly unknown. We have made it through more than one mental health practitioner. We have made it through depression and him feeling suicidal to him being able to express self-love and happiness. We made it, and you can make it too. Even when your teen makes you believe they don't need you, they 100% do. They need your support and guidance more than ever. I never thought my child would need me more as a teenager than when he was little, but here we are, and we both have grown so much together.

I like to refer to the problematic period a teenager will inevitably go through as the night of the teenager or here in the Midwest we call it a rough patch. This period could be short, long, or in my case around two years. Since every teen is different, with different needs, exposures, and coping skills, no one can really predict the length or severity of their struggle. What I can tell you is our story and hope that it helps the people who need to hear it.

It started in seventh grade. My son had chosen to go to a magnet middle school that focused on science and math as those are his areas of interest. The school was in a rougher area of town, but other children were being bused there for years for the same purpose. He was doing well in school, no negative communication from his teachers or administration and he even gotten student of the month award halfway through the year. On paper, he looked great.

He has always been an introverted and intellectual child. He would play by himself growing up or hang out one-on-one as opposed to groups of children. As the year progressed, I noticed small changes. He was becoming more withdrawn, hanging out in his room more and not talking as much. He seemed more irritable and quiet. He didn't want hugs anymore. Every day I would ask him about his day, phrasing it in different ways to try and get an answer. Every answer was vague. I would ask about friends, and he would say he talked to people at school and hung out. I would try to give him hugs or touch his shoulders affectionately, and he would dodge me. I read about moody teenagers, and I didn't know if that was what was causing the changes in his behavior or something more.

It was my first time raising a teen, and I truly felt at a loss.

Towards the end of seventh grade one day he became angry out of nowhere over a simple problem. He was in a rage, and I had never seen him like this, ever. Once I was able to get him to calm down and sit, I told him he had to tell me what was wrong.

What he said completely shocked me and until this day I will never forget the despair in his voice or on his face.
He told me, "I don't want to live anymore, if life is like this, then what is the point."

My baby felt hopeless and very much emotionally overwhelmed. I told him he wasn't alone and that I loved him unconditionally. I acknowledged his feelings and offered my help. I told him how proud I was for him telling me. I asked him to help me come up with a plan because we have the ability to ask others for help. So we called his school psychologist and left a message that we needed an emergency meeting for him and safe plan for school.

We had a group meeting with all his teachers, and not a single one had a clue that he was suicidal. He seemed normal to them, no red flags.

What I found out from that meeting also left me reeling. Over half of those teachers were quitting because of the toxic mob-like mentality of the students at the school. They spend more time disciplining students than actually teaching. One teacher said she was suicidal that year too and had started anti-depressants.

I found out how my child had been bullied. They cursed at him and called him things, "ugly and stupid." They trapped him in the bathroom and hit him. They threatened him and would punch or kick him. Hit him on the back of the head when they walked by him. They would do this on the bus and at school. I asked my son, who was an active second-degree brown belt in kickboxing and jiu-jitsu at the time why he never hit back. He told me there was always more than one at school and on the bus, it was a girl, and they would record it. He was afraid to defend himself, and his anxiety was through the roof.

He had prolonged abuse from his peers. He was alone and an easy target. No one knew. I was angry and upset for a long time. How could I not know? I was an involved parent. I gave him a stable home life. I asked questions; I took him to do fun things. We went for drives, and I gave him plenty of chances to talk to me without judgment. I gave him affection and love even when he pushed me away. I set up outings with my friends who had kids around the same age. The signs were slow and subtle, but they were still there.

How did everyone miss them?

I felt as though everyone, including myself, had failed him. We got him the help he needed to process his traumatic events, and we moved school districts. He is now at a school he loves and has a great peer group.

During this difficult period, you will cry and yell and feel more frustrated than ever. You will feel like you are not reaching your child and that at that moment, there is an immense fear of the unknown, what will happen?

There. Is. No. Control.
There is only showing up for your child consistently. Focus on the now and giving them positive support and unconditional love. Get them the help they need and know that not every mental health practitioner is a fit for your child. All of it is hard, but you will navigate it together. It gets better, and then one day, you will see a strong, happy, and resilient young adult emerge from the shadows. They will shine a bright light onto the world, and you couldn't be more proud.

Please know as a parent, you are not alone. During one time or another, we are all trying to parent a struggling teen.

The Miracle of the Age Gap
Karen Gauvreau

"When the parenting road is smooth, celebrate. Don't waste a minute dreading the next curve. Glance over at your teenager often. Steal glimpses of who they are becoming. Maybe even hug them if you're feeling really brave." ~Lightly Frayed

My husband and I will never be empty nesters. By the time we drop our youngest off at college, we'll drive straight to the retirement home, unpack our bags and pick up our Bingo cards.

We didn't set out to have a large age gap in our family. But after having three kids within four years, we welcomed a pause. A much-needed pregnant pause, without the pregnant. Many days felt like an exhausting episode of Survivor. I wished someone would vote me off the island so I could shower and take a nap. Adding another child to our family was the furthest thing from our minds.

But as I approached my fortieth birthday, my perspective unexpectedly shifted. My arms suddenly ached for one more baby — a sweet little Now-Or-Never. Soon after, I waved a positive pee stick at my beaming husband, so grateful for this blessing.

One Sunday morning in the church lobby, we began sharing the news that we were expecting a fourth blue bundle. Eyebrows shot up as people sized up the three boys we already had, ages ten, eight and six. "Yeah - our parents only have one recipe, X-Y," explained our middle son.

And he was not wrong.

The day after giving birth to Landon, I received my first glimpse into multitasking with a preteen and a newborn. As I snuggled into bed to nurse our baby, a stressed voice whispered from my doorway. "Mom. I need help with my Math test, that's tomorrow." Ayden laid out his books and set up camp at the foot of my bed. I quizzed him on polygons, contentedly dozing off between questions.

It will be okay.

We found our groove and adjusted to our busy rhythm. Our big kids were a huge help with our little one. The older three could get themselves ready and even help with the baby — such a contrast from a few years earlier when simply leaving the house required military precision. The ten-year-old rocked and settled his baby brother better than my husband and I some days. Friends marveled at how comfortably Ayden walked, swayed and cradled his brother, unfazed by newborn cries. If Landon was cranky, I was excited for the school bell to ring so my assistant would return.
All our boys had a remarkable relationship with their little brother. He was the puppy they always wanted, minus the Kibbles and Bits. There was solidarity amongst our family as we celebrated every baby milestone.

"Mom - Landon just rolled over!"

"Dad. Record this. I taught Landon how to sit up for three seconds."

"Landon just said my naaaaaaaaame!"

This little one generated more ooooohs and aaaaahs than a summertime fireworks display. Landon was toted to every school event and performance and shown off proudly to friends and teachers.

One day all four kids waited at the table while I began serving dinner. And a competition ensued.

Ayden: "Hey, Landon - Who's your favorite brother?"

Landon: "I don't know."

Liam: "It's me, right? Don't you remember when Rylan wouldn't let you have the green cup?"

Rylan: "Or what about the time Ayden wouldn't let you watch your favorite show. That was mean, right?"

With twinkling eyes, they jockeyed for position, bantering and bringing up offenses committed by their brothers, in order to win Best Sibling that day.

This was the variety of life with a wide age range. Never a shortage of babysitters. Never a dull moment. And as our little Caboose grew, so did the hilarity.

Teen: Can I have a hug?

Landon: Um. No.

Teen: Please?

Landon: Nope.

Teen: If you give me a hug, I'll let you play with my leg hair.

Landon: Oh. Okay. T'anks.

Truly the strangest win-win.

Of course, all parents expect hills and valleys. But what I hadn't anticipated was the timing of our valleys. Almost overnight, we simultaneously hit intense stages. Teens, practically-teens, and a toddler while Mom teetered on the threshold of menopause. A whole different range of fireworks lit up our home as big feelings exploded. One disappointing text message, a Netflix loading error, or a crashed Lego tower could send sparks flying.

As CEO, I had parental whiplash some days. From achoos to curfews; picky eating to endless eating; sleep training to drivers training. Navigating this dizzying array created rather unique dinner conversations. Potty training and the hazards of pot. First words and watching our words. Skipping naps and skipping class.

But no matter the day, our children provided me with options. If a teenager was moody, I snuggled the toddler. And if the toddler had a tantrum, a teenager offered a sympathetic smile and knowing chuckle, being careful not to reboot the tantrum. And if all age groups were struggling, I'd send out an SOS to my husband to hurry home.

I had thought the greatest advantage of having space between our kids might be having help with the youngest. Someone to push him on the swing or read him a bedtime story. But I discovered the real value exceeded my expectations, especially in the life of one of our older boys.

During a particularly bumpy patch, one of our teens barely looked at us. The distance seemed to arrive without warning, and as he worked through his struggles, he put up high walls, we weren't allowed to scale. His hard gaze felt painfully personal since we had always been close.

Trusted friends kept reminding me that our boy was still there, wanting to be close but no longer sure how to show it. During this time, I kept a picture of the two of us on my bedside table to remind me of the simple days when he leaned his chubby cheek into mine, grinning widely. I needed that precious smile to end my days as we navigated this rocky stage.

After a particularly tense morning, the distance overwhelmed me, my hidden tears threatening to appear. Knowing this would only annoy him, and make the situation worse, I struggled to strike the right balance, to find the right topic of conversation. But every attempt ended poorly.

Throughout this prickly patch, our teenager still went to church early most weeks with my husband to practice keyboards for the service. I would pull up the second vehicle an hour later with the rest of the group in tow.

And that's when I saw it.

Our teen caught sight of his youngest brother running towards him down the middle aisle. Dropping his guard, he flashed the most genuine smile I had seen in a long while. As the facade fell, I glimpsed my man cub's sweet self again. His teenage muscles flexed as he bent down, scooped up his brother and kissed him on the cheek. Landon's legs wrapped around his hero, fitting his big brother's arms as comfortably as he had in those early days. And in an instant, it was clear who most needed the hug; who needed this brotherly bond to fall back on; who needed a safe person to break through the distance. And the teary Mama watching this sacred moment? She inhaled peace again. It will be okay.

In this moment of clarity, I discovered one secret to surviving the teenage years.

Keep a little one close by. Or a puppy. A puppy would work too.

The Teenage Years Are Tough
Gina Low

"Teens have become immune to death stares and raised voices. Want best behavior for twenty-four hours? Say I don't have time right now, but we need to have a talk tomorrow." ~Shes Overflowing

OOOH, Teenagers. Their two-year-old selves stole your heart long ago, and now you cannot believe that this girl with your eyes and her dad's cheekbones is really telling you off. She has boobs on her chest and car keys in her hand (both of which you gave her!), and she really has the nerve to tell you to "relax a little." Yeah mom, relax a little. After all, you should totally be relaxed about opening grades that have also just SCREAMED very loudly that you must be the worst mother in the world.

I did fall in love with their two-year-old selves. Well, three and five to be exact. You see, I am a step-mom. A bonus mom, second mom, step-monster, wicked witch of the west…whatever you want to call me. It really doesn't bother me, I've heard it all. The fact remains that I stepped in to be all of these things when their bio-mom wouldn't. Couldn't. Didn't. I dealt with pull-ups and immunizations and leading girl-scout troops…and, although I did not manufacture them in my body, I can still look at them and see my minis. While noticing their father's cheeks, I also hear the perfectly correct use of the word "regardless." I see #1 holding the keys in her hand exactly as I've shown her, fist around the bundle with one sticking out to protect herself. I notice that #2 has finally found the perfect shade of "not orange spackle" foundation and that she is taking my well-intended advice on that fruity perfume. I may not be a direct match for an organ transplant, but these girls are mine.

2013 was my worst, and last fight ever with #1. She was almost fifteen. I can't even remember if it was over grades or the condition of her room or what, but it was bad. My girl had some behavioral issues - caused in part I'm sure by maternal abandonment, and maybe in part by a chemical imbalance, and DEFINITELY in part by hormones! It didn't matter; they were our storms to ride out.

I'm not going to sugar-coat it even a little; it was a scene out of a Lifetime movie. We'd had similar scenes before, although they had become fewer and farther between. Imagine two toddlers crying in the background because the screaming is too loud. Imagine an enraged teenager who feels so little control over the situation that she resorts to using the only thing she CAN control, her physical being.

Imagine a younger sister corralling her brothers to go outside and play so they can all pretend this isn't happening. I'd said it before, but this time I meant it. The next time this happens, I have to call the police. For the safety of everyone in our home, I have to call the police.

As I said, that was my last fight ever with #1. I'm not sure if she believed me about the police that time, or if it was her hormones finally settling. Maybe she just finally realized that I was here to stay, and not just as her father's wife. We went from "can't be in close quarters for too long" to best friends in what seems to be a blink of an eye. Suddenly, I had the pleasure of walking along-side this beautiful teen creation on her journey into adulthood. We worked through the excitement (and let-down) of her first crush, and shopped for formal wear, and shared ice cream in front of Christmas movies right after Halloween. If she was out and saw something that she knew I'd love, she'd leave me a little surprise on the counter.   When she had friends over for a game night, she wanted me to be there playing right along with them. (Okay, she wanted her dad there too…but this story is about me!)

Fast forward to 2018. My first-born daughter graduated high school with honors and worked hard through a shoulder injury to get into the Navy. Her injury prohibited her from her first choice of serving capacity, but she didn't let that stop her from chasing her ultimate dream of becoming a nurse. Through rehab and PT and insurance docs and waivers, she was finally able to enlist. During her time at boot camp, she earned a spot on the special recruit division with her respectful, diligent attitude and three years of JROTC. After her first schooling, she earned a second and was high enough in the class rankings to choose her duty station. I can't tell you where she's stationed, but I can tell you it does involve Hazardous Duty Pay (every mom's dream, right?!). It's a beautiful destination, surrounded by water and sunshine. The location allows her to vacation in places she's never even dreamed of. The location allows her to try new foods, learn new cultures, and become more of an independent woman than I had ever imagined. The location also has GOLD…beautiful, inexpensive GOLD, and very talented jewelers. Like the many other little gifts she's left me, my daughter met a jeweler and thought of me. Because secrets are not her strong suit, she had to call me; she was so excited!

My #1, my first-un-born daughter, had a mother's ring made for me. It holds every birthstone in our family, and I cannot wait to have it on my finger.

So hang tight, mommas. The teenage years are tough. They will require a hefty supply of wine or chocolate, probably both. One day they can't walk without holding your hand, and the next they wouldn't be caught dead holding your hand. Use that time to hold on tight with both hands – brace yourself in your faith, your marriage, and your friendships – and hold on tight.

And one day, just like that, they'll be back to ask for your hand (and not just a hand-out!).

They will need your hand to help them move.

They will need your hand to wipe their tears.

They will need your hand to high-five when they get their first promotion, and they will need your hand to hold as they labor through childbirth.

If you're lucky like me, they will ask for your hand to give you one of the most meaningful representations of the beauty you've worked so hard to create.

About the Authors

Jelise Ballon is an educator, writer, and speaker. She is author of the non-fiction book *Forgiven & Restored* by Eliezer Tristan Publishing. Her writing has been featured on *The Today Show*, *Her View from Home*, *Motherly*, *Inspire More*, and others. She lives with her husband and three children in the Shenandoah Valley. You can read more at her blog: www.neitherheightnordepth.com

Marybeth Bock, MPH, is Mom to two college students and one delightful hound dog. She has logged time as an Army wife, childbirth educator, college instructor and freelance writer. She lives in Arizona and thoroughly enjoys research and writing - as long as iced coffee is involved. You can find her work on *Grown and Flown*, *Blunt Moms*, the *Scottsdale Moms Blog*, *Teen Strong AZ*, and on random scraps of paper around her house.

Lyndee Brown is Haden and Ryland's mom. She has been married to her husband Matt for ten years. She has a bachelor's of science degree and works as a Respiratory Therapist during the day. At night she moonlights as Superwoman. She is very fluent in sarcasm and can burn toast with the best of them.

Shannon Carpenter is a humorist that lives in Kansas City, Mo where his three children keep him constantly entertained. He enjoys long walks with his dog and explaining to his wife that he is done having any new children. Represented by Chris Kepner.

Christine Carter writes at TheMomCafe.com, where she hopes to encourage mothers everywhere through her humor, inspiration, and faith. Her work is published on several various online publications and she is the author of the books, *Help and Hope While You're Healing: A Woman's Guide toward Wellness While Recovering from Injury, Surgery, or Illness* and *Follow Jesus: A Christian Teen's Guide to Navigating the Online World*. Both sold on Amazon.

Judy Daniell resides in Nebraska with her crew of raucous teens and her high school sweetheart. She enjoys reading, writing, traveling and cheering for these boys...which is where you'll find her spending most her of her time. You can read more of her writing at www.judydaniell.com

Shannon Day is co-author of the book *Martinis & Motherhood: Tales of Wonder, Woe & WTF?!*, a collection of funny and heartwarming stories (plus easy-to-make martinis) for moms. Shannon lives in the Toronto area with her husband and their three daughters. You can find her words at several online sites as well as in print Connect with Shannon Day on Facebook. https://www.facebook.com/martinisandmotherhood/

Whitney Fleming is a freelance writer, social media consultant and exhausted mom to three beautiful teenage daughters. She tries to dispel the myth that she is a typical suburban mom although you can always find her in a minivan driving her kids to soccer practices and cello lessons. Follow her on Facebook and Instagram @PlaydatesonFridays

Karen Gauvreau is a freelance writer at *Lightly Frayed*. She would squeeze her four-baby-body into a cheerleader's uniform for you to know someone is rooting for you as a Mom - cartwheeling for your victories and offering a pep talk when you feel pummeled. And if you're parenting one teen or a few, she's got you. Connect with her on *Lightly Frayed* on Facebook – for tips on raising teens you are crazy about.

Lynne Getz is a married mom of three living in the outskirts of Philly whose life can be summed up in six words: this is not what I planned. Her first child was born with a rare chromosome disorder, so she became a different kind of mom than she ever expected. She started her blog, *Like a Mother*, to show other moms that motherhood and martyrdom are not synonymous, that self-care is not selfish, and that having a child with multiple disabilities does not mean you have to sacrifice your goals--you just have to adjust them. In addition to writing and speaking, she runs a multimillion dollar direct sales team, dabbles in public television and podcasting, and tries her best to teach her younger children to be good people.

Valli Gideons is a military bride, who writes about raising kids with hearing loss, military life, and other things from the heart. The mother of two thriving teens, she shares what she has learned throughout their journey in a raw, honest way. Unrelated but not irrelevant...With a degree in journalism, she wrote her first short story in second grade about a walking/talking sponge (Hello, *SPONGEBOB*); She's been an exercise instructor since her teen years (*Flashdance* sweatshirts, leg warmers, and vinyl records to prove it); and may have been an extra on the vintage nineties hit, *Beverly Hills 90210* (proof still found on VHS tapes). She is still besties with her two closest pals from elementary school, who encouraged her to share her story. She hopes by sharing her journey, she can offer a sliver of inspiration for anyone who is entering or in the midst of their own fog. You can find her work on mybattlecall.com and on Facebook and Instagram @mybattecall

Cheryl Gottlieb Boxer is a New Jersey-based writer and college advocacy coach for an education non-profit. She writes about raising teens and parenting while chronically ill. Her writing has appeared on *TODAY Parents*, *Your Teen for Parents*, *Scary Mommy*, *Motherly*, *Kveller*, *The Mighty*, as well as in other online and print publications. Cheryl blogs about micromanaging her husband, children, and confounding cockapoo at *No Sick Days for Mom*. (www.cherylgottliebboxer.com).

Jennifer Hurvitz is known for her no-nonsense approach to dating after divorce. She's a relationship coach, best-selling author, and host of the *Doing Divorce Right Podcast*. Happily divorced since 2014, Jennifer lives in Charlotte with her two teenage boys. Through her popular blog, *The Truth Hurvitz*, and weekly podcast, Hurvitz helps people understand what a happy divorce can look like and how to dip their toes back into the dating world. She loves sharing her insight on how to stay in a successful marriage too! Reach out via jenniferhurvitz.com if you'd like her to speak at your next event. Follow Jennifer on Instagram, Facebook, Twitter, and LinkedIn. Grab her books on amazon.com, barnesandnoble.com, and warrenpublishing.net.

Marcia Kester Doyle is the author of the humor book, *Who Stole My Spandex? Life in The Hot Flash Lane*, and the voice behind the midlife blog, *Menopausal Mother*. Her work has appeared in *The New York Times, The Washington Post, McSweeney's, Cosmopolitan, Good Housekeeping, AARP, Country Living, Woman's Day*, and *House Beautiful*, among others. She lives in sunny south Florida with her husband, four adult children, and two feisty granddaughters.

Heather LeRoss is an imperfect human trying to raise two perfect humans who embarrasses herself frequently, loves big, fails a lot, eats too much chocolate, and spends too much on purses. Her first book, *Just Tell Me I'm Pretty; Musings on a Messy Life* has won two awards and was written to allow women a break from reality; a chance to laugh, cry, and feel all the feels while reading her words. She's currently working on her next book, a work of fiction.

Lisa Leshaw is the co-author of the book, *How Are You Feeling Mama? (You Don't Need to Say, "I'm Fine")* She is anxiously stepping into semi-retirement, while continuing to conduct her empowerment workshops for women. If anyone is interested in hiring an old grandma, please give her a call.

Gina Low is a mom, wife, youth sports cheerleader, and wine taster who swears that the forties are the best years of her life! She writes for her fellow warriors who may have temporarily lost themselves in the throes of spit up and Goldfish. She will help guide you through the years of cleats, cups (every cup but sippy cups anymore), and collective bargaining with teens; all while reminding you that your oxygen mask must come first!

Anne Metz works part time as a freelance writer and spends the other part getting kids off the bus, breaking up fights, doing laundry, and cleaning up after her son and triplet daughters. She is passionate about sharing her struggles to let others know they aren't alone in this journey of motherhood. Her work has been featured on *Her View from Home, Today Parenting, Scary Mommy*, and *Perfection Pending*. You can find more of her writing on her blog: www.onceuponamom.net

Tiffany O'Connor is the originator, author, and co-editor of *The Unofficial Guidebook to Surviving* series. She is the writer behind the popular blog #lifewithboys. Her work appears in several anthologies, including *Chicken Soup for the Soul My (Kind of) America*. Tiffany is a mom to two amazing, energetic, and fearless human boys and two loveable furry boy dogs. She is married to her high school sweetheart and has three college degrees. Her hobbies include watching television shows about zombies, hiding in her hot tub with a glass of champagne, and listening to Taylor Swift songs on repeat.

Elyse Orecchio is an adventure seeker in NYC who can't stay still even though she's always yawning. She works in nonprofit communications and writes about theatre and travel. She holds fierce pride for Queens, where she lives with her husband and personal photographer Joe, her magical kids Theo and Melody, three cats, and lots of scratched up furniture. eorecchio@gmail.com @elyseorecchio

Renee Robbins is a Midwestern-based writer, mother, and part-time curmudgeon. She's been published in *Cosmopolitan, Marie*

Claire, The Elephant Journal and others. She lives in Kansas with her husband, two children and six cats and is NOT writing a book. But she thinks about it a lot.

Katie Smith had three kids in three years and crafts her ass off in order to stay sane. She loves to write, wear faux leather pants, eat at burger joints, and make beautiful things. She pays her kids to rub her feet and play with her hair.

Shelby Spear is a sappy soul whisperer, sarcasm aficionado, pro-LOVE Jesus adoring mom of three Millennials writing stuff & doing life with hubs of twenty-six years. She is the co-author of the book, *How Are You Feeling, Momma? (You don't need to say, "I'm fine.")* You can read her open heart about the revelations, screw-ups, gaffes, and joys of motherhood on her blog shelbyspear.com, around the web, and in print at *Guideposts*.

Elizabeth Spencer is mom to two daughters (one teen and one young adult) who regularly dispense love, affection, and brutally honest fashion advice. She blogs about faith, family, and food (with some occasional funny thrown in) at *Guilty Chocoholic Mama* (http://guiltychocoholicmama.blogspot.com/). She also writes for *Her View from Home, Grown and Flown, Your Teen for Parents,* and Crosswalk.com. In her spare time (namely, when she's not chauffeuring her younger daughter around), Elizabeth volunteers as a band mom, facilitates women's Bible study, sings on her church worship team, and bakes chocolate chip cookies that cover a multitude of maternal sins.

DC Stanfa is an expert at fun and its byproduct, trouble. She the author of *The Art of Table Dancing: Escapades of an Irreverent Woman* and co-editor of the anthology, *Fifty Shades of Funny: Hookups, Breakups, and Crackups.* Her work has been featured in several of the Erma Bombeck Workshop publications, including the 2018 anthology *Laugh Out Loud: 40 Women Humorists Then and Now…Before We Forget.* Stanfa has mentored women and girls in business, as well as the arts. She facilitated a creative self-expression program for the Boys & Girls Club and taught humor writing workshops in conjunction with Scholastic.

Jodie Utter is a freelance writer and the creator of the blog, *Utter Imperfection*. From the backdrop of the Pacific Northwest, she works to connect stories of struggle and overcoming hardship to encourage others to feel less alone and more at home in their hearts, minds, and relationships. You can connect with her on Facebook, Instagram, & Twitter—where she tells the raw truth about life and love and the hope that can always be found, even though.

Letter from the Editors

Thank you for reading this book. We hope that you loved it. We were so lucky to have an amazing squad of outstanding writers agree to join us on this journey. I hope they all know how much we appreciate each and every one of them. If you enjoyed their stories in this book make sure you check out their blogs, Facebook pages, Twitter feeds, fabulous Instagram posts, and awesome books.

This book was created with the goal of showing what it is really like raising teenagers. As you can tell from our stories, every young person is unique and special in his or her own way, and every parent is just trying to do their best. If you feel like it is tough and if you are afraid that you are not doing it correctly… you are not alone. We all feel that way sometimes. Just take a deep breath and know that you are doing a good job (I know that because you care enough to read parenting books like this one)

If you found this book to be hilarious, heartwarming, and relatable, we would love it if you told your friends about it and we would be extremely grateful if you would take the time to write a review on Amazon.

Make sure to check out all of the other fabulous **books** in *The Unofficial Guidebook to Surviving* series.

XOXO,
Tiffany & Lyndee

www.ingramcontent.com/pod-product-compliance
Lightning Source LLC
LaVergne TN
LVHW041629070426
835507LV00008B/529